Prenn and Fosha remind us that we are all continuous learners in every human exchange. This volume carefully maps AEDP supervision principles and practices and, most importantly, brings to life the human connections that are vital to the development of transformative experiential psychotherapy and the supervision that flows from within it.

—**Douglas Braun-Harvey, MFT, CGP, CST,** The Harvey Institute, San Diego, CA, and author of *Sexual Health in Recovery: A Professional Counselor's Manual*

AEDP has been one of the most exciting developments in our field in recent decades. Like AEDP itself, this book is deeply experiential, offering a vivid sense of AEDP practice and how it is supervised. Readers experience being right there in the room as supervision is conducted by a master clinician.

—**Paul L. Wachtel, PhD,** CUNY Distinguished Professor, Doctoral Program in Clinical Psychology, City College of CUNY, New York, NY, and author of *Therapeutic Communication, Second Edition: Knowing What to Say When*

From the developer of AEDP together with one of AEDP's top trainers comes a book on the process of AEDP supervision that parallels the powerful approach itself. Prenn and Fosha offer supervisees the same intense experiences they offer clients, and so the learning is deep and transformative.

—**Richard C. Schwartz, PhD,** Department of Psychiatry, Harvard Medical School, Boston, MA, and developer of the Internal Family Systems Model of psychotherapy

Supervision Essentials for

Accelerated Experiential Dynamic Psychotherapy

Clinical Supervision
Essentials Series

CLINICAL SUPERVISION ESSENTIALS

HANNA LEVENSON *and* ARPANA G. INMAN, Series Editors

Supervision Essentials for

Accelerated Experiential Dynamic Psychotherapy

Natasha C. N. Prenn
and Diana Fosha

American Psychological Association • Washington, DC

Published by
American Psychological Association
750 First Street, NE
Washington, DC 20002
www.apa.org

To order
APA Order Department
P.O. Box 92984
Washington, DC 20090-2984
Tel: (800) 374-2721; Direct: (202) 336-5510
Fax: (202) 336-5502; TDD/TTY: (202) 336-6123
Online: www.apa.org/pubs/books
E-mail: order@apa.org

In the U.K., Europe, Africa, and the Middle East, copies may be ordered from
American Psychological Association
3 Henrietta Street
Covent Garden, London
WC2E 8LU England

Typeset in Minion by Circle Graphics, Inc., Columbia, MD

Printer: Maple Press, York, PA
Cover Designer: Mercury Publishing Services, Inc., Rockville, MD

The opinions and statements published are the responsibility of the authors, and such opinions and statements do not necessarily represent the policies of the American Psychological Association.

Library of Congress Cataloging-in-Publication Data
Names: Prenn, Natasha C. N., author. | Fosha, Diana, author. | American
    Psychological Association, publisher.
Title: Supervision essentials for accelerated experiential dynamic
    psychotherapy / Natasha C. N. Prenn and Diana Fosha.
Other titles: Clinical supervision essentials series.
Description: Washington, DC: American Psychological Association, [2017] |
    Series: Clinical supervision essentials series | Includes bibliographical
    references and index.
Identifiers: LCCN 2016037886 | ISBN 9781433826405 | ISBN 1433826402
Subjects: | MESH: Object Attachment | Psychotherapy—education |
    Psychotherapy—methods | Clinical Competence
Classification: LCC RC489.P72 | NLM WM 460.5.O2 | DDC 616.89/14—dc23
LC record available at https://lccn.loc.gov/2016037886

British Library Cataloguing-in-Publication Data
A CIP record is available from the British Library.

Printed in the United States of America
First Edition

http://dx.doi.org/10.1037/0000016-000

Contents

Foreword to the Clinical Supervision Essentials Series

We are both clinical supervisors. We teach courses on supervision of students who are in training to become therapists. We give workshops on supervision and consult with supervisors about their supervision practices. We write and do research on the topic. To say we eat and breathe supervision might be a little exaggerated, but only slightly. We are fully invested in the field and in helping supervisors provide the most informed and helpful guidance to those learning the profession. We also are committed to helping supervisees/consultees/trainees become better collaborators in the supervisory endeavor by understanding their responsibilities in the supervisory process.

What is supervision? Supervision is critical to the practice of therapy. As stated by Edward Watkins[1] in the *Handbook of Psychotherapy Supervision*, "Without the enterprise of psychotherapy supervision, ... the practice of psychotherapy would become highly suspect and would or should cease to exist" (p. 603).

Supervision has been defined as

> an intervention provided by a more senior member of a profession to a more junior colleague or colleagues who typically (but not always) are members of that same profession. This relationship
>
> - is evaluative and hierarchical,
> - extends over time, and

[1] Watkins, C. E., Jr. (Ed.). (1997). *Handbook of psychotherapy supervision.* New York, NY: Wiley.

- has the simultaneous purposes of enhancing the professional functioning of the more junior person(s); monitoring the quality of professional services offered to the clients that she, he, or they see; and serving as a gatekeeper for the particular profession the supervisee seeks to enter. (p. 9)[2]

It is now widely acknowledged in the literature that supervision is a "distinct activity" in its own right.[3] One cannot assume that being an excellent therapist generalizes to being an outstanding supervisor. Nor can one imagine that good supervisors can just be "instructed" in how to supervise through purely academic, didactic means.

So how does one become a good supervisor?

Supervision is now recognized as a core competency domain for psychologists[4,5] and other mental health professionals. Guidelines have been created to facilitate the provision of competent supervision across professional groups and internationally (e.g., American Psychological Association,[6] American Association of Marriage and Family Therapy,[7] British Psychological Society,[8,9] Canadian Psychological Association[10]).

---

[2] Bernard, J. M., & Goodyear, R. K. (2014). *Fundamentals of clinical supervision* (5th ed.). Boston, MA: Pearson.

[3] Bernard, J. M., & Goodyear, R. K. (2014). *Fundamentals of clinical supervision* (5th ed.). Boston, MA: Pearson.

[4] Fouad, N., Grus, C. L., Hatcher, R. L., Kaslow, N. J., Hutchings, P. S., Madson, M. B., . . . Crossman, R. E. (2009). Competency benchmarks: A model for understanding and measuring competence in professional psychology across training levels. *Training and Education in Professional Psychology, 3* (4 Suppl.), S5–S26. http://dx.doi.org/10.1037/a0015832

[5] Kaslow, N. J., Rubin, N. J., Bebeau, M. J., Leigh, I. W., Lichtenberg, J. W., Nelson, P. D., . . . Smith, I. L. (2007). Guiding principles and recommendations for the assessment of competence. *Professional Psychology: Research and Practice, 38,* 441–51. http://dx.doi.org/10.1037/0735-7028.38.5.441

[6] American Psychological Association. (2014). *Guidelines for clinical supervision in health service psychology.* Retrieved from http://www.apa.org/about/policy/guidelines-supervision.pdf

[7] American Association of Marriage and Family Therapy. (2007). *AAMFT approved supervisor designation standards and responsibilities handbook.* Retrieved from http://www.aamft.org/imis15/Documents/Approved_Supervisor_handbook.pdf

[8] British Psychological Society. (2003). *Policy guidelines on supervision in the practice of clinical psychology.* Retrieved from http://www.conatus.co.uk/assets/uploaded/downloads/policy_and_guidelines_on_supervision.pdf

[9] British Psychological Society. (2010). *Professional supervision: Guidelines for practice for educational psychologists.* Retrieved from http://www.ucl.ac.uk/educational-psychology/resources/DECP%20Supervision%20report%20Nov%202010.pdf

[10] Canadian Psychological Association. (2009). *Ethical guidelines for supervision in psychology: Teaching, research, practice and administration.* Retrieved from http://www.cpa.ca/docs/File/Ethics/EthicalGuidelinesSupervisionPsychologyMar2012.pdf

The *Guidelines for Clinical Supervision in Health Service Psychology*[11] are built on several assumptions, specifically that supervision

- requires formal education and training;
- prioritizes the care of the client/patient and the protection of the public;
- focuses on the acquisition of competence by and the professional development of the supervisee;
- requires supervisor competence in the foundational and functional competency domains being supervised;
- is anchored in the current evidence base related to supervision and the competencies being supervised;
- occurs within a respectful and collaborative supervisory relationship that includes facilitative and evaluative components and is established, maintained, and repaired as necessary;
- entails responsibilities on the part of the supervisor and supervisee;
- intentionally infuses and integrates the dimensions of diversity in all aspects of professional practice;
- is influenced by both professional and personal factors, including values, attitudes, beliefs, and interpersonal biases;
- is conducted in adherence to ethical and legal standards;
- uses a developmental and strength-based approach;
- requires reflective practice and self-assessment by the supervisor and supervisee;
- incorporates bidirectional feedback between the supervisor and supervisee;
- includes evaluation of the acquisition of expected competencies by the supervisee;
- serves a gatekeeping function for the profession; and
- is distinct from consultation, personal psychotherapy, and mentoring.

The importance of supervision can be attested to by the increase in state laws and regulations that certify supervisors and the required multiple supervisory practica and internships that graduate students

---

[11] American Psychological Association. (2014). *Guidelines for clinical supervision in health service psychology.* Retrieved from http://www.apa.org/about/policy/guidelines-supervision.pdf

in all professional programs must complete. Furthermore, research has confirmed[12] the high prevalence of supervisory responsibilities among practitioners—specifically that between 85% and 90% of all therapists eventually become clinical supervisors within the first 15 years of practice.

So now we see the critical importance of good supervision and its high prevalence. We also have guidelines for its competent practice and an impressive list of objectives. But is this enough to become a good supervisor? Not quite. One of the best ways to learn is from highly regarded supervisors—the experts in the field—those who have the procedural knowledge[13] to know what to do, when, and why.

Which leads us to our motivation for creating this series. As we looked around for materials that would help us supervise, teach, and research clinical supervision, we were struck by the lack of a coordinated effort to present the essential models of supervision in both a didactic and experiential form through the lens of expert supervisors. What seemed to be needed was a forum where the experts in the field—those with the knowledge *and* the practice—present the basics of their approaches in a readable, accessible, concise fashion and demonstrate what they do in a real supervisory session. The need, in essence, was for a showcase of best practices.

This series, then, is an attempt to do just that. We considered the major approaches to supervisory practice—those that are based on theoretical orientation and those that are metatheoretical. We surveyed psychologists, teachers, clinical supervisors, and researchers domestically and internationally working in the area of supervision. We asked them to identify specific models to include and who they would consider to be experts in this area. We also asked this community of colleagues to identify key issues that typically need to be addressed in supervision sessions. Through this consensus building, we came up with a dream team of 11 supervision experts who not only have developed a working model of supervision but also have been in the trenches as clinical supervisors for years.

---

[12] Rønnestad, M. H., Orlinsky, D. E., Parks, B. K., & Davis, J. D. (1997). Supervisors of psychotherapy: Mapping experience level and supervisory confidence. *European Psychologist, 2,* 191–201.

[13] Schön, D. A. (1987). *Educating the reflective practitioner: Toward a new design for teaching and learning in the professions.* San Francisco, CA: Jossey-Bass.

We asked each expert to write a concise book elucidating her or his approach to supervision. This included highlighting the essential dimensions/key principles, methods/techniques, and structure/process involved, the research evidence for the model, and how common supervisory issues are handled. Furthermore, we asked each author to elucidate the supervisory process by devoting a chapter describing a supervisory session in detail, including transcripts of real sessions, so that the readers could see how the model comes to life in the reality of the supervisory encounter.

In addition to these books, each expert filmed an actual supervisory session with a supervisee so that her or his approach could be demonstrated in practice. APA Books has produced these videos as a series and they are available as DVDs (http://www.apa.org/pubs/videos). Each of these books and videos can be used together or independently, as part of the series or alone, for the reader aspiring to learn how to supervise, for supervisors wishing to deepen their knowledge, for trainees wanting to be better supervisees, for teachers of courses on supervision, and for researchers investigating this pedagogical process.

ABOUT THIS BOOK

In this book, *Supervision Essentials for Accelerated Experiential Dynamic Psychotherapy*, Natasha C. N. Prenn and Diana Fosha make it clear that accelerated experiential dynamic psychotherapy (AEDP) supervision is a psychotherapy-based model; as such, the transformative supervisory process in AEDP parallels the transformative therapeutic process in AEDP. Although AEDP comes out of a psychodynamic psychotherapy tradition, it has replaced psychodynamic concepts, such as confrontation and psychopathology, with concepts of affirmation and privileging the positive, and a healing orientation.

The AEDP therapist strives to cocreate with the client "a new experience and have that experience be good," as stated in the Introduction. Similarly, the AEDP supervisor relies on AEDP principles of change to cocreate with the supervisee an experience in which they deal with challenging situations together, and that experience also should be good.

Using affective resonance, pressuring with empathy, and dyadic affect regulation in the here-and-now, supervisors cocreate emotional safety with their supervisees. The focus is on having the supervisory relationship begin to function as a secure base. Through experiential–dynamic work, the supervisor then proceeds to help supervisees process overwhelming emotional experiences, which results in increased resiliency from which to help their clients. Lest the reader think that the AEDP model of supervision can be characterized as a warm-and-fuzzy approach—au contraire. The approach is skill based: Supervisees learn how to help their clients have authentic, core affective experiences through learning skills, such as moment-to-moment tracking, recognition of somatic markers, microanalysis of videotaped therapy, and use of a "map" of therapeutic steps and processes. Paraphrasing Fosha, supervisees learn how to "feel and deal."

This book will expose you to the nuts and bolts of AEDP supervision emanating from developmental, attachment, neurobiological, and research underpinnings. From transcripts of actual supervision sessions along with detailed commentaries by Prenn and Fosha, the reader will see how supervisees come to embrace this model. And, as a special treat, Prenn and Fosha introduce the book by inviting the reader on an experiential journey into AEDP supervision. We think you will enjoy the ride!

We thank you for your interest and hope the books in this series enhance your work in a stimulating and relevant way.

Hanna Levenson and Arpana G. Inman

Acknowledgments

We start our acknowledgments with Hanna Levenson. The excitement of meeting and working with Hanna on the Accelerated Experiential Dynamic Psychotherapy (AEDP) Fidelity Scale and finding such a like-minded intellect and champion of AEDP to boot was contagious and productive. Then, her invitation to us to participate in this groundbreaking APA series on supervision was an honor and a delight. We have both learned and benefited from her rigor, precision, and matter-of-fact kindness. She has been there at every stage of the way guiding this book and its accompanying DVD on AEDP supervision. We are so grateful.

Michael Glavin jumped into the fray of this project, and could not have been a more enthusiastic, capable, and willing supervisee. We want to thank him for taking such a big risk to come in as such an already accomplished therapist and letting himself be vulnerable enough to learn and demonstrate how we teach and grow in AEDP. And all of this on tape! Kudos, Michael.

It would be hard to imagine a more gifted and generous group of clinicians and colleagues than the AEDP Institute faculty. Throughout the pages of this book, you will hear the echoes of many rich and illuminating conversations we have had collectively as a faculty and in seemingly infinite combinations of dyads and groups. This acknowledgment does not start to do justice to their contributions to the AEDP model of supervision.

We both want to thank and acknowledge all of the experiential assistants who have volunteered at Immersion and Essential Skills courses. They have given us their time and their hearts and minds, and have worked tirelessly to improve our trainings. Their belief in and commitment to the power of AEDP and AEDP training has been transformational for so many. We could not teach experiential–dynamic therapy without them.

A number of people read part or all of several earlier versions of this book. Natasha Prenn would like to thank Judy Rabinor, Jessica Slatus, Molly Morgan, Jan Bowman, and her husband, Stelios Vasilakis. Her daughter, Emma Prenn-Vasilakis, read, proofread, queried and greatly improved the manuscript. Diana Fosha wishes to thank Karen Kranz and Hilary Jacobs Hendel, who helped with communicating essence in fewer words and shorter sentences.

Natasha Prenn is also grateful to her close friends for their everyday support: Lisa Lupinacci, Amy Ostergaard, Maggie and Greg Schwed, and Hilary Jacobs Hendel.

And a big shout out to Viktor Koen not only for his AEDP diagrams but also for his humor and his AEDP *true other* way of being: "My dear, I am always just a phone call away!"

Diana Fosha's main thanks go to her coauthor, Natasha Prenn. Her tireless enthusiasm for making AEDP's theory and practice teachable and doable is the heart and ethos of this book. Diana also thanks her own past supervisors for teaching her so much about what's important to do and also what's important to not do in supervision. She tries to be true to both sets of lessons.

Supervision Essentials for

Accelerated
Experiential
Dynamic
Psychotherapy

Introduction

Healing-oriented and attachment based, accelerated experiential dynamic psychotherapy (AEDP) is a comprehensive, integrative, and transformative model of psychotherapy. Its fundamentally experiential approach synthesizes attachment research, emotion theory, experiential ways of working, developmental models, trauma studies, body-focused treatments, and affective neuroscience into a coherent theoretical framework that informs both therapy and supervision.

AEDP supervision is a psychotherapy-based model that has emerged from AEDP theory and clinical practice. Supervisees develop AEDP skills and increase their relational and affective capacities through the experience of AEDP and by learning specific techniques described in this book.

Until now, the transmission of how to practice AEDP has been from supervisor to supervisee and from teacher to student, and through the

http://dx.doi.org/10.1037/0000016-001
Supervision Essentials for Accelerated Experiential Dynamic Psychotherapy, by N. C. N. Prenn and D. Fosha

collective viewing of videotapes in seminars, workshops, and supervision groups. This book provides a foundation for and articulates the basic principles that inform AEDP supervision. Here, for the first time, we unpack its methodology—not only to guide supervisors seeking how to best help supervisees learn AEDP but to help supervisees change and develop so that they can be more effective psychotherapists. Clinicians come to AEDP because they want to change the way they work and be transformed. AEDP faculty around the world teach through showing videotapes of AEDP psychotherapy sessions and documenting transformations, big and small. Given emotion contagion (Hatfield, Cacioppo, & Rapson, 1992) and resonance phenomena (Siegel, 2010), right-brain-to-right-brain communication (Schore, 2009), and mirror neurons (Rizzolatti & Craighero, 2004), we know that many therapists come into AEDP supervision and training already having a *felt sense* (Gendlin, 1981, 1996) of the AEDP transformational experience; that is, they already know in a visceral way the AEDP change process (Fosha, 2000a, 2009a). Once they have had this experience, they want more of it and want to learn how to work in this way with their clients.

In this Introduction, we provide a brief overview of the historical origins of an AEDP approach to supervising and describe the salient issues in treatment and supervision. We also describe each of our own pathways to becoming an AEDP supervisor. Diana Fosha's clinical journey is synonymous with her path to developing AEDP, so she has detailed the progression of her training and her responses to that training. Natasha Prenn's clinical and supervisory trajectory, which has grown out of Fosha's work, parallels the expansion of the AEDP Institute and its trainings. Then we describe the readership for whom this book is intended and offer readers a chapter-by-chapter road map to the rest of the book.

ORIGINS OF AEDP SUPERVISION

AEDP officially was born in 2000 with the publication of Diana Fosha's (2000b) book *The Transforming Power of Affect: A Model for Accelerated Change*. After the creation of the AEDP Institute in 2005, the growth of the AEDP model has expanded in two ways: (a) by contributions from the institute faculty and certified supervisors, some of which are reflected in their publications—Anne Cooper, Ron Frederick, Kari Gleiser, Yuko Hanakawa, Hilary Jacobs Hendel, Jerry Lamagna, Ben Lipton, David Mars, Miriam Marsolais, Jenna Osiason, Karen Pando-Mars, SueAnne Piliero, Eileen Russell, Steve Shapiro, Jessica Slatus, Barbara Suter, Dale Trimble, Gil Tunnell, and Danny Yeung—and (b) by contributions of those who have conducted research on AEDP: Conceição, Iwakabe, Edlin, et al. (2016); Faerstein and Levenson (2016); Iwakabe and Conceição (2015, 2016); Lee (2015); Piliero (2004); and Schoettle (2009).

AEDP's name and initial letters pay tribute to its early lineage in psychodynamic psychotherapy and short-term dynamic psychotherapy (STDP; Malan, 1999), and then in the transformation from STDP to intensive short-term dynamic psychotherapy (ISTDP; Davanloo, 1990, 2000). From STDP and especially ISTDP, AEDP understands and lives by the transforming power of affect. However, AEDP replaces the ISTDP focus on confrontation and intrapsychic crisis with the concepts of dyadic affect regulation (Fosha, 2000b, 2001), pressuring with empathy (Russell, 2015), affirmation (Fosha, 2000a), and privileging the positive (Fosha, 2000a; Russell, 2015; Russell & Fosha, 2008), among other things. Most fundamentally, STDP and ISTDP's pathology-based orientation is fundamentally supplanted by AEDP's foundational healing orientation. With the shift from ISTDP to AEDP comes a move from an understanding of symptoms and maladaptive patterns—that is, the stuff that brings people to seek therapy—as reflections of psychopathology and self-punishment (Davanloo, 1990; Della Selva, 1996) to an appreciation of them as reflecting fundamentally adaptive processes. When viewing symptoms as healthy best efforts that, nevertheless, are inadequate to meet the challenges of thwarting environments, it is easy to see how a neutral confrontational stance should be supplanted by a "together with," affirmative, explicitly empathic, emotionally engaged, "we're in it together" stance.

These principles of AEDP all come to life in AEDP supervision. As we describe in the chapters that follow, the focus on healing and on undoing aloneness, the strategies of affirmation, and privileging the positive are key aims and interventions of AEDP supervision.

TREATMENT MODEL AND SUPERVISORY MODEL

Attachment theory and research currently are front and center in the conversations about psychotherapy, and yet, when clinicians turn to the literature to learn how to practice an attachment-informed therapy—seeking to put theory and research into clinical practice, they find little written guidance about how to be a good enough attachment figure. What specifically do you do and say in your sessions to bring about earned attachment security? This question is even more apparent in supervision: What are the actual skills you need as a supervisor to be experienced as an earned-secure attachment figure by your different supervisees? What kinds of things might you say and do to work in this way? AEDP's supervisory model responds to and offers guidance to precisely these questions.

AEDP clinicians strive to help the client have a new experience and have that experience be good (Fosha, 2002). All subsequent work, understanding, learning, and restructuring of existing expectations and dynamics are rooted in that initial positive, transformative experience. Similarly, we want the supervisee to traverse a new or challenging situation together with a caring, engaged other, and we want that experience to be good. The subsequent work of learning theory and interventions—and the many how-tos—is rooted in the positive experiences of the supervision.

We often read that safety and attachment—the secure base—need to be in place before further work can be done. AEDP argues that corrective emotional and relational experiences in therapy and in supervisory sessions themselves create earned-secure attachment (Prenn, 2009; Wallin, 2007) and change in attachment status over time. Secure attachment doesn't precede the work of supervision; rather, it comes out of the work of supervision. We seek to establish a secure attachment relationship from the get-go by leading with supervisor risk-taking—our self-disclosures, and vulnerability (Fosha, 2006; Lipton & Fosha, 2011; Prenn, 2009)—which allows the supervisee to take more risks and, in this way, the work becomes deeper. As the supervisor and supervisee are able to traverse increasingly challenging moments together, the relationship becomes more solid, allowing both to take even more risks, so that the "thickness" of the relationship increases (Tronick, 2003, p. 479).

As discussed in Chapter 1, AEDP understands psychopathology as being the result of unwilled and unwanted aloneness in the face of over-whelming experiences (Fosha, 2000b). Lacking support in which one's resources are just insufficient to the task, the individual becomes reliant on short-term solutions (i.e., protective mechanisms or defenses), which do the job of ensuring survival in the short run but produce constriction and distortion (i.e., psychopathology) when relied on over the long term. To transform psychopathology and restore access to adaptive emotions, the AEDP therapist above all seeks to undo the client's aloneness. With support and dyadic affect regulation in place, the client can relinquish his or her reliance on defenses and can begin to risk genuine emotional experiencing, knowing that he or she has a supportive, emotionally engaged other with whom to share the suffering and the joys. All that holds true for an AEDP client holds true for our supervisees.

PATHWAYS TO AN AEDP MODEL

Diana Fosha

My initial training was in psychoanalytic theory. Given the bent of my graduate program, City University of New York's doctoral program in clinical psychology, and the nature of my own interests, I entered the field studying psychoanalytic theory with a strong developmental orientation. I was immersed not only in Freud and other classical analysts but also in Ferenczi, Suttie, Guntrip, Winnicott, Searles, and Kohut, and in the developmental work of Piaget and that of Mahler, Pine, and Bergmann. They remain influential in my thinking to this day. However, the length of psychoanalytic treatment and the relative selective inattention to issues of effectiveness and evidence made me uncomfortable.

Enter STDP, first via the work of David Malan (1999), then ISTDP by way of the work of Habib Davanloo. The appeal of Malan's work was his stated intention and goal to preserve the depth and intensity of psychodynamic treatment but shorten its length and increase its effectiveness. Key aspects of Malan's work that are implicit in AEDP to this day are the ability to maintain a tight focus while staying closely attuned to the client and the close moment-to-moment tracking of the material according to the categories of the triangle of conflict (which became restructured and renamed in AEDP as the *triangle of experience*; see Chapter 1). This now famous triangle is in the process of being renamed the *change triangle* by Hilary Jacobs Hendel (in press), tipping its hat to the purpose of our work to change or help make a shift from anxiety and defense to core feeling. In 1979, however, Malan had a conversion experience when he witnessed the power of Davanloo's model of ISTDP (Davanloo, 1990, 1995).

ISTDP became the next station on the path that eventually culminated in the development of AEDP and the publication of *The Transforming Power of Affect* (Fosha, 2000b). Separate from Malan's extraordinary endorsement, what personally drew me to Davanloo's work was the power of the affective phenomena systematically evoked by his techniques, and the rapidity with which visceral experiences of deep emotion were accessed and worked through to a transformative result from the first session onward. In addition, he taught, presented, and supervised from videotapes of actual therapy sessions, and would only supervise trainees who would present their own therapy work from videotapes of their sessions.

I trained with Davanloo for 3 years. It was a powerful, if difficult, training. However, my next wave of discomfort, now with ISTDP, continued to spur what became the eventual development of AEDP. Two areas of profound unease permeated my experience: The first was the aggressively confrontational nature of the work with defenses in ISTDP; the second was that ISTDP theory, such as it was, did not do justice to the transformational power of the experiential phenomena to which the techniques yielded access.

My quest became twofold. First, I wanted to see if it were possible to have the same rapid access and powerful emotional phenomena yielded by ISTDP work if the therapist and client engaged defense work as allies and partners, rather than as adversaries in a confrontation or a battle. Second, it was important to me to have a theory that accounted for the powerfully transformational effects of affective phenomena that could be systematically elicited once the effect of the defenses was minimized. Initially, I engaged in the first quest with a group of colleagues led by Michael Alpert (1992), with whom I joined forces from 1988 to 1993. During that time, Alpert and

I also worked in close and collegial collaboration with Leigh McCullough (1997; McCullough et al., 2003). The second quest, namely, that powered by transformational phenomena in search of a theory, was my own.

Working together with and in parallel to both Alpert and McCullough, our shared struggle was to preserve the essence of Davanloo's therapeutic effectiveness—the power of visceral experience and the capacity to get to it quickly, from the initial moments of the first encounter with the client—while evolving a more supportive, kinder, yet effective user-friendly mode of relating that could hold the deep affect work. Gradually, we were able to switch from the "head-on collision" stance (Davanloo, 1990, p. 7) that involves radical challenge and pressure to relinquish maladaptive defenses to a therapeutic stance of radical empathy and emotional engagement. We moved beyond the metaphor of a head-on collision with a client's resistance and defenses to a therapeutic stance, the aim of which was to "melt" the client's defenses through empathy. This stance involves helping the client feel safe in a relationship with an emotionally engaged therapist, thereby minimizing the need for defenses. After an amicable parting of ways between Alpert and me, that stance continued to evolve in my work, increasingly informed by developmental research into caregiver–infant interactions and attachment theory.

AEDP's subsequent relational techniques flow from a stance of explicit empathy, care, and compassion instead of challenge, pressure, and relentless confrontation. Through this stance, a paradigm shift occurred: The focus was radically switched from ISTDP's focus on what is wrong to AEDP's focus on what is right and away from ISTDP's pathology-oriented model to AEDP's healing-oriented model.

The quest to develop a rigorous explanatory metapsychology for the transformative experiential work that resulted from the rapid bypassing of defenses was mine. From 1995 to 2000, the same spiraling process that describes AEDP's metatherapeutic processing described the 5 years of gestation and labor in birthing AEDP theory. In attempting to account for the transforming power of the affective phenomena that emerged once the effect of defenses was minimized, I went to emotion theory, beginning with Charles Darwin (1872/1965) and William James (1902/1985), and proceeding to Tomkins (1962), Ekman (1984), and other current emotion theorists. To account for the power of the relationship and the moment-to moment processes of attunement, disruption, and repair, I reengaged my developmental roots, which had been nurtured in my graduate clinical psychology program, while keeping the videotaping of clinical sessions and the focus on the visceral experience of core affective phenomena and their adaptive sequelae.

In particular, I reengaged attachment theory and research that then were and now continue to be in a renaissance (e.g., Fonagy & Target, 1998; Main, 1995, 1999), as well as the work of developmentalists or "baby watchers" (e.g., Beebe & Lachmann, 1988, 1994; Emde, 1981, 1983, 1988; Stern, 1985; Stern et al., 1998; Tronick, 1989; Tronick, Bruschweiler-Stern, Harrison, et al., 1998). The resonance between the baby watchers studying videotapes of parents and their children engaged in moment-to-moment dyadic interaction and the therapists studying videotapes of therapists and their clients engaged in their moment-to-moment dyadic interactions did not escape me. A lot of ecological validity existed between the two. My studies and attempts to integrate them in my writing energized my attunement to the phenomena of clinical work. What I experienced, videotaped, and studied during the day in my clinical practice I would try to research and understand—through the lens of various readings—at night at home. This process of going back and forth between phenomena and reflection—with increased understanding leading to noticing new phenomena and with new phenomena requiring and thus leading to new theoretical integration and development—is how what came to be called AEDP was born.

I applied it in therapy, and then, as AEDP started to become known and clinicians wanted to learn it, I applied it to supervision.

Natasha Prenn

I came to psychotherapy and AEDP from an earlier career as a teacher of Latin and Ancient Greek language and literature. In my transition from teacher to psychotherapist, I was struck again and again by how little teaching of actual clinical skills was included in most of my clinical training. I often asked, "But what do I say and what do I do?" I felt that

I had entered a field that was rich in theory and rather lacking in clinical application. In May 2004, I saw Diana Fosha's work at an attachment conference. My immediate reaction on a left-brain intellectual level was that the theory behind the clinical practice made complete sense to me. It was the translation of neuroscience into clinical practice grounded in reliably occurring natural phenomena. It was an aha moment, one of those moments accompanied by the click of recognition and a sense of rightness. In a visceral right-brain way, I knew deep down that this was how you helped clients change. This was how to be an attachment therapist. I had found a theoretical and clinical home base, and I was hooked.

After taking Fosha's AEDP Immersion course in the summer of 2004, I entered individual and group supervision with Ben Lipton and flew to San Francisco to take Ron Frederick's core training. I began studying Fosha's transcripts and videotapes for the structure of the magic I was experiencing in her work. She had already begun to articulate in her theoretical writings techniques: ways of being (i.e., stance) and ways of doing and intervening (i.e., specific language). I started collecting AEDP interventions and studying their sequencing in her work and in the work of other AEDP therapists. Working experientially was like learning a new language. I catalogued interventions, and then I practiced using these interventions in my own sessions with my clients. Gradually, I gathered and catalogued the most effective interventions for me and, with this vocabulary and language in place, I experimented and found my own personal voice in the structure and language of AEDP.

In this process, the development of a focus on the experiential language of AEDP and the teaching of specific foundational interventions became the backbone of what is now a 2-year-long AEDP Essential Skills course in AEDP. For information about AEDP training, consult https://www.aedpinstitute.com, the AEDP website. As I taught and supervised AEDP, I found that an essential component of learning was in the language of interventions: Trainees needed the words of actual interventions to answer their questions: "What do I say now?" and "What do I say next?" These are the questions I had experienced in my own training. Foreign language learning directly parallels the experience of change we try to promote in AEDP supervision and therapy, in which there is no established neural network for a skill or competency; we need experience and to put language to that experience to express ourselves, to communicate what we know that viscerally we want to do. One of my contributions to AEDP to date is this *languaging* and cataloging of how-to interventions, that is, the translation of AEDP theory into specific, easily learnable and integrated steps and sequences. I am now known for my "How to AEDP" and "Nuts and Bolts of AEDP" workshops.

In addition to playing a central role in developing the curriculum for the 2-year-long Essential and Advanced Skills courses, I supervise therapists through the AEDP certification process and train therapists to assist at the Essential Skills course. I also supervise AEDP supervisors-in-training and mentor AEDP therapists who are developing new workshops and presentations. I worked on the AEDP Fidelity scale (see https://www.aedpinstitute.org/wp-content/uploads/2014/01/AEDP-Fidelity-Scale-Self-Report.pdf) and, as cofounding editor of *Transformance: The AEDP Journal*, with Kari Gleiser, I helped expand AEDP theory and practice. This monograph, with its articulation of how to supervise in AEDP, is a natural extension of all of this.

Like Fosha, I had received no academic training as a supervisor when I began supervising. As an educator and teacher, I came to the job of AEDP supervisor equipped with teaching tools and, of course, the tenets of how to work with the supervisory relationship from AEDP therapy. I owe a huge debt to my first supervisors in AEDP: Diana Fosha, Ben Lipton, and Ron Frederick. Unlike Fosha, I was fortunate to have such talented, kind, and generous AEDP supervisors to emulate, imitate, and learn from.

AEDP supervision, like AEDP therapy, is bidirectional and affects both or all members of the therapeutic dyad or triad. Supervisors and teachers of AEDP can attest that we have been profoundly changed for the better because we have had, and continue to have, the privilege of being supervisors and teachers of AEDP. We grow professionally and personally because of the inherent recursive experiences of deep emotion, relatedness, and transformation, repeatedly witnessing and working with the videotaped work of supervisees and clients. The same phenomenon, increased by orders of magnitude, also takes place at AEDP training sessions and workshops in which whole groups of practitioners, through

watching videotapes of transformative therapy, experience vicarious healing, state sharing, and expanded states of consciousness (Tronick, 1989,
2009; Tronick et al., 1998), and are powerfully transformed.

AUDIENCE FOR THIS BOOK

This book is intended for supervisors and supervisees, whether they are in
graduate school, clinics, or private practice, and for psychotherapists, psy-
chiatrists, social workers, psychologists, counselors, marriage and family
therapists, and teachers. This book also is important reading for dynamic,
relational, and interpersonal psychotherapists who want to learn how to
supervise in a more experiential, attachment, emotion-focused manner.
Being profoundly integrative, AEDP's approach to supervision will be
useful to graduate students and experienced clinicians of many different
orientations. Given the current interest in attachment and in interpersonal
neurobiology, AEDP's phenomenology-based approach to supervision and
therapy—and its emphasis on verifiability and thus the centrality of video
recording in both therapy and supervision—is likely to make it appealing
and useful to different psychotherapy orientations.

OVERVIEW OF THIS BOOK

In Chapter 1, we introduce the key theoretical underpinnings to AEDP
therapy and supervision, and introduce the first two prongs in our three-
pronged approach to supervision: the knowledge and capacities of AEDP
supervision. Chapter 2 is dedicated to the role of the relationship in AEDP
and demonstrates the skills needed and the language of interventions to
put all of this into immediate action. Chapter 3 offers an immersion in the
AEDP supervisory experience via the microanalysis of a video recorded
supervision session with Fosha and supervisee, Michael Glavin.[1] The
full session is available for viewing on the DVD *Accelerated Experiential*

---

[1] With the exception of Michael Glavin, who agreed to be quoted in this book, the identities of all other
supervisees and clients who appear in this work have been disguised to protect confidentiality.

Dynamic Psychotherapy (AEDP) Supervision (Fosha, 2016) from American Psychological Association Books at https://www.apa.org/pubs/videos/ 4310958.aspx. Chapter 4 addresses practical issues, including different formats of supervision, documentation, and evaluation. Chapter 5 outlines how to deal with differences in supervisees, from attachment styles to their different levels of experience. Chapter 6 answers the question "Who will guard the guards themselves?" (*Satires VI* by Roman poet Juvenal; trans. Clausen, 1992). The chapter focuses on the training and care of supervisors. We close with a chapter about the research supporting our model of supervision, followed by a suggested reading list, if you find yourself wanting more.

1

Key Concepts

The aim is to maximize time spent in positive attuned interactions and the positive affects that accompany them, and to as rapidly as possible metabolize the negative affects associated with misattunements and disruptions, so as to restore coordination and positive affective experience. The positive tone of the relational experience is crucial. Positive vitalizing experiences and positive dyadic interactions are the stuff of secure attachment, the stuff of resilience, and the stuff of growth and expanding health and mental health (Fosha, 2009b; Fredrickson, 2001; Lyons-Ruth, 2006; Russell & Fosha, 2008; Schore, 2001). (Lipton & Fosha, 2011, pp. 260–261)

This chapter introduces the key concepts of accelerated experiential dynamic psychotherapy (AEDP) supervision. However, in keeping with AEDP's experiential approach, we introduce AEDP supervision

http://dx.doi.org/10.1037/0000016-002
Supervision Essentials for Accelerated Experiential Dynamic Psychotherapy, by N. C. N. Prenn and D. Fosha

by showing it in action before telling you why we are doing what we are doing. Let yourself read, and if that feels okay to you, have a visceral, right-brain experience. Trust, though, that after these vignettes, we spend the rest of the chapter describing in detail the key concepts, knowledge, and capacities of AEDP to satisfy your left brain, thus filling in the gaps in your declarative, theoretical knowledge. Let yourself have an experience of AEDP supervision in action.

VIGNETTE 1: THE OPENING MOMENTS OF A FIRST SUPERVISION SESSION

A new supervisee arrives in the supervisor's (i.e., Prenn's) office. Her hands tremble a little as she pulls her notebook and computer out of her bag. She bites her lip. As her AEDP supervisor, what am I to do? The theory and clinical practice of AEDP supervision inform the supervisor's decision from this first face-to-face interactional moment. The supervisor's stance in these interactions is almost exactly how she is as an AEDP therapist: welcoming, leading, anxiety regulating, explicitly helpful, self-disclosing, normalizing, and on the lookout for strengths to affirm.

Supervisor[1]: Our first meeting, huh . . . mmm . . . anxiety . . . [**This is explicitly moment-to-moment tracking; the supervisor lets the supervisee know that she notices her anxiety: she is leading and wanting to help.**]

Supervisee: Ya, I was surprised on my way over here. I found myself getting nervous.

Our first task in AEDP supervision is to undo aloneness (Fosha, 2000b, 2009b). Just as AEDP's credo is that we want our clients to have a new experience with us—and we want that experience to be good (Fosha, 2002)—in parallel fashion, supervisors want our supervisees to have a

---

[1] In the transcripts in this book, nonverbal behaviors are indicated in italic type within brackets. Our microanalyses of the supervisory interventions and their effect are indicated in bold type within brackets.

new experience with us and we want that experience to be good from the first moments of our work together. Our relationship and the experiences within it are integral, fundamental, and foundational to supervisee learning. Learning is significantly impaired, even impossible, if anxiety is too high. The supervisee's anxiety needs to be regulated, and we need to start to cocreate safety so that the supervisory relationship can begin to function as soon as possible as a secure base (Bowlby, 1988) in our newly forming attachment relationship. Once we start to cocreate safety and the supervisory relationship is becoming a secure base, then we can launch explorations. That is where the stretching and the new learning occur!

Supervisors want our supervisee to have an experience with us. Then, whatever experience we—supervisor and supervisee—have had, we also want the supervisee to know that he or she has had that experience. We call this *metatherapeutic processing*, or *metaprocessing*, for short (more about this concept later in the chapter). To clarify, we want the supervisee to experience something—something maybe new and definitely good— understand what happened, and also have words for what he or she has now deeply felt. The ability for the supervisee to articulate what he or she has felt facilitates integration; it will help the supervisee to translate his or her experience in supervision into therapeutic actions with clients.

Although a number of different ways are available to undo aloneness, create safety, regulate anxiety, and make the implicit experience explicit and relational—and we describe them in detail shortly—one invariably reliable way to achieve all of them in one fell swoop is self-disclosure (Bromberg, 1998, 2006, 2011; Farber, 2006; Jourard, 1971; Maroda, 1998, 2004, 2009; Prenn, 2009; Wallin, 2007). That's what the supervisor does next:

Supervisor: Oh, I remember my first AEDP supervision. I was anxious, too! [**self-revealing, normalizing**]
[*The supervisee smiles, makes fleeting eye contact, and lets out a big exhale.*]

In AEDP, the unit of intervention has two parts: the intervention itself and how it is received by the supervisee. So, the next step after the supervisor's intervention—her self-disclosure—is its metaprocessing. Having disclosed something personal and vulnerable about herself, she wants to know how the intervention lands with the supervisee and how the supervisee is affected by it:

Supervisor: How is it to know this about me . . . that I was anxious, too? [**Supervisor metaprocesses her self-disclosure.**]

New supervisees usually are relieved to find that they are not the only ones to feel that way. Learning that the authority figure also sometimes feels anxiety and, not only that, but that he or she is also willing to share it, can be powerful. Nevertheless, rather than assume or try to guess at how the intervention is received, we keep the interactions experiential and see precisely and specifically how *this* person is reacting to *this* supervisor's intervention in *this* moment:

Supervisee: I feel better.

Supervisor: Ya? What's it like? Is it okay to ask you that? [**asking permission**]

Supervisee: Yeah, ya, ya. . . .

Supervisor: You have a sense of yourself inside/in your body/physically? What do you know inside about "better?" Again, is it okay with you to ask you this? [**somatic focus: asking permission**]

Supervisee: Yes, it is okay to ask. Yes. Let's see: a shift. Calmer . . . more here . . . better [*smiles*].

Supervisor: Mmm. A smile [*nods*].

Supervisor: You have a real sense of yourself. How nice to know that. [**affirms and makes the interaction explicit**]

Supervisor: How is it . . . how are we doing? We are just starting. How is it to share this with me? [**metaprocesses and makes the experience relational**]

The supervisor is starting by putting an AEDP tenet into immediate action in AEDP supervision: privileging the new and good experience from the get-go (Fosha, 2000a) and also tending explicitly to the supervisory dyad's relationship. AEDP supervisors work experientially and relationally all the time. The supervisor is introducing that this is how we like to work and is explicitly asking permission to work in this way. It is modeling—explicitly giving the supervisee a visceral experience of AEDP's attachment-based, experiential dynamic work.

The supervisor's self-disclosure is authentic and also is a technique: Her vulnerability helps a supervisee be with his or her vulnerability—the inevitable vulnerability of supervision—and be more okay with it. The supervisor immediately works to normalize anxiety in supervision. She says, "Me, too!" As we know, "disclosure begets disclosure" (Jourard, 1971, p. 16), which means the process can then deepen. The supervisor is trying to make this experience collaborative and mutual, and, most of all, safe enough. She is the supervisor. It is her office. She has enough authority. The supervisee cannot be expected to open up and be vulnerable in a productive, learning-enhancing way if the supervisor keeps herself hidden.

In the same way that a tenet of AEDP is that we cannot expect a client to rapidly open up to a therapist who remains aloof (Fosha, 2000b). This holds true for supervision. This supervision hour is in the service of the supervisee's goal to learn how to do AEDP therapy. All the work supervisors do, including the disclosures we make, is in the service of undoing aloneness, establishing our relationship as a secure base, and cocreating a good experience from the beginning. The experiential dynamic focus in supervision provides the transformative tools that guide our supervisees. We use these standard AEDP techniques explicitly and with permission, contracting and recontracting around personal material and our relationship as we go. Metaprocessing is a way of rigorously and systematically checking in about the process itself; it keeps the relationship as safe as possible and on track.

In the preceding short vignette, we introduced an example of the relational and experiential nature of AEDP supervision. It demonstrates clearly how supervisors work from the first moments of the supervisory hour to create the conditions for the supervisory relationship to develop as a secure attachment relationship. All supervisory relationships are potentially attachment relationships wherein insecure, avoidant, anxious, and secure attachment dynamics can play themselves out.[2] We want to explicitly cocreate this relationship as an earned-secure attachment relationship (Pearson, Cohn, Cowan, & Cowan, 1994; Roisman, Padrón, Sroufe, & Egeland, 2002; Wallin, 2007).

One of the main tasks of AEDP supervision is to cocreate a meaningful connection with the supervisee and imbue this contact with a new experience of acceptance, enjoyment, mutuality, and success. The aim is to cocreate a bidirectional relationship (it feels good and promotes growth in the supervisor, too) in which the lion's share of the supervisory dyad's time together is spent in positively valenced interactions.

In the interview that follows the supervision session described in the DVD *Accelerated Experiential Dynamic Psychotherapy (AEDP) Supervision* (Fosha, 2016), available from American Psychological Association (APA) Books at https://www.apa.org/pubs/videos/4310958.aspx, Hanna Levenson, the host of the APA Psychotherapy Supervision series, asks the supervisee, Michael Glavin, a question: "How is this AEDP supervision different, for you, from other supervisions you've had?"

Michael: "Fundamentally, it just *feels good* [*smiles*]. Like, a supervision that feels good . . . not just in the affirmation—the overt affirmation—but also in the delight of the supervisor in the supervisee's work . . . so the delight, the curiosity, the togetherness—the feeling like we're doing this *together* . . . the risk-taking . . . right, and then the . . . overcoming the risks, and doing it, and having some success moments, and processing—that just . . . feels really good to be a part of . . ." [*nods*].

Positive experiences that are explicit and reflected on in supervision, that is, are metaprocessed, are safety engendering and risk inspiring. They are conducive to thriving and the emergence of the best version of the clinician as supervisee and therapist. Affirmation, moment-to-moment tracking,

---

[2] See Chapter 5 for working with different attachment styles in AEDP supervision.

and the accurate reflection of all we see lead to moments of recognition in which the supervisee is accurately mirrored and recognizes him- or herself in what we see. Recursive experiences of being seen and recognized create the robust confident self of the AEDP supervisee that translates into action in therapy sessions (Fosha, 2009a—also reprinted in *The Neuropsychotherapist* and available online at https://www.aedpinstitute.org/wp-content/uploads/2015/09/2009_Fosha_Neuropsychoth.pdf) and, as you will see in the next vignette, those experiences tend to feel good, vital, and enlivening, even in the context of high-wire risk-taking.

SAFETY AND EXPLORATION, OXYTOCIN AND DOPAMINE

We do not learn, explore, or dare to take risks when our nervous system is in a state of defensive physiological reactivity. We need safety first; only then can we explore. When we do, and that goes well, too, as in the example that follows, the contagious and vitalizing positive affects experienced by both partners fuel the dyadic system with energy, which feels good and fuels further exploration and risk-taking (Fosha, 2009a, 2013c).

When we think about learning new things and taking the risk of changing the way we work as therapists, we are in the realm of Bowlby's (1982) exploratory behavioral system, Panksepp's (Panksepp & Biven, 2012) seeking system, and of playfulness à la Dan Hughes (2007). Exploring, seeking, and playing are perhaps as crucial for our adaptation and survival as safety. It is through our explorations into the world that we grow, learn, and become increasingly versatile. For exploration to be productive and creative, we must carry it out with zest and vitality, and it must be motivationally driven. That's where we need to go beyond oxytocin to understand the power of dopamine and dopaminergic systems in the brain (Fosha, 2013c), and their crucial role in transformational experiences in therapy and supervision.

Research on oxytocin has shown it to be an essential ingredient that contributes to experiences of safety, connection, and compassion (Carter, 1998; Carter & Porges, 2012; Porges, 2009). Research also has shown that many experiences that lead to learning, memory consolidation, and expansion of the self as a result of new experiences and new learning are mediated by dopamine (Murty & Adcock, 2013; Panksepp & Northoff, 2009; Shohamy & Adcock, 2010). Dopamine is the neurotransmitter that fuels the self's seeking system in its search for experiences that feel good and right because, when we feel good, we are open to learning. What makes AEDP so different from other ways of working is that we work to stay with and return as quickly as possible to these oxytocin- and dopamine-rich, open-to-learning states that have a positive valence. We privilege the positive and know that "nothing that feels bad is ever the last step" (Fosha, 2004, 2009b; Gendlin, 1981, p. 29). When we have a rupture in our supervisory relationship, we keep going until we repair it, until mutual coordination and enjoyment are back on track (Safran & Muran, 2000; Tronick, 1998). The experience of successful re-coordination is a dopamine-rich and often new experience.

Our next vignette shows how safety allows risk-taking, and how risk-taking, when met with support, affirmation, and genuine engagement, leads to new learning, which, in turn, leads to positive vitalizing, mutually enlivening, and expansive experiences.

VIGNETTE 2: RISK-TAKING, AFFIRMATION, METAPROCESSING, POSITIVE STATE-SHARING

Midway through the supervision session, a challenging moment occurs in the therapy that the supervisee (i.e., Michael Glavin) is presenting to me (i.e., Fosha), his supervisor. As a supervisory dyad, we already have done some work so that by now, the client is known to both of us. Safety also has already been well-enough established through the supervisory transactions that precede this moment, much of it created by my explicit recognition and affirmation of the supervisee's good work. The result is a drop-down to a different level of relational safety that then allows the supervisee, Michael, to take a risk. In the dialogue that follows, Michael courageously starts off by saying he "doesn't know what to do" at this particularly difficult junction in the session with his client Amy.

Supervisee: And then . . . and I see her now starting to collapse again, like she's . . . it's not making sense [to her], and then tears come up, and so she seems to be getting dysregulated, right?

Supervisor: Right.

Supervisee: Um . . . So I don't know what to do [*laughs*]. So, like, what you'll see next [in the video of the session] is sort of me just reflecting that back, like trying to make that explicit of what I see happening.

Supervisor: Right. I appreciate—

Supervisee: If you have a different—yeah, I'd be interested to hear a different way to work here, in this moment where she goes to that "but, it's not gonna make sense," and then she starts to get dysregulated . . .

Supervisor: Right. I wanted to just appreciate, you know, your honesty, and your being direct about "I don't know what to do . . ." [**transformance detection,**[3] **affirmation**]

Supervisee: Yeah.

Supervisor: 'Cause, I mean, we all feel that. [**supervisor self-disclosure, normalizing**] We all feel that, you know, there's so much going on, the client's dysregulating . . . There are several things, and that's that sort of internal sense, so your being able to share that with me, I really appreciate that. [*Michael smiles, nods.*] Yeah. I think it took courage. You know, particularly we're on tape and everything like that, so . . . it even ups the ante, so it took even more courage. [**affirmation**]

Supervisee: [*smiles wider and gives a small laugh*] I appreciate you saying that.

Supervisor: Yeah. So, can you stay with that—just for a second? [**quintessential invitation to deepen the experience, with permission to stay with experience of affirmation; a time limit—"just for a second"—makes it**

---

[3] *Transformance*, the motivational drive toward healing and self-righting, is defined first in the interview segment that follows this supervision vignette. It also is defined more formally later in this chapter.

safer for supervisee] What it's like to have me say, you know—I mean, first of all, we all struggle with that . . . [**metaprocess affirmation, then self-disclosure**]

Supervisee: Right.

Supervisor: Like, those moments, like "uuuhhh" [*winces*]. [**The wince suggests an implicit self-disclosure, that is, "I know what that feels like."**]

Supervisee: Right.

Supervisor: It's not just an intellectual question, but, secondly . . . it's a brave thing to do [*nods*]. [**Repeats the affirmation. Checking for receptive capacity: Can the supervisee receive the affirmation?**]

Supervisee: [*nods*] [**His head nod signals he is ready to receive it.**] Mmm. It feels like I'm recognized and being seen, and validated, in both the "aaah" like that part, but also like, yeah, the sharing of it, feels good. I'm glad I did [share it].

Supervisor: Yeah. Just for one moment [**another boundaried time limit for a potentially stressful new experience**], just, if you stay with . . . [*using hand, gestures in a circle around chest*] it's feeling good, 'cause it's a little paradoxical, right . . . It's something that's hard but, yet, it feels good. [**another round focusing on the body with nonverbal communication; teaching moment: something that is hard feels good when shared**]

Supervisee: Right. It feels relaxing in here [*using hand, makes same circular gesture over chest*], and calming openness. [*Both nod.*] Excitement.

Supervisor: Yeah. When you said that, I actually felt myself [*makes similar hand gesture and takes deep breath*] take a breath and drop down. [**supervisor's self-disclosure of supervisee's impact on her; dyadic regulation through nonverbal channels**] All right, shall we go back to Amy? [**Mission accomplished; the challenging moment was met and transformed. Now it is time to return to the next round of work and view another segment of the therapy session**]

The next day, series host Hanna Levenson interviews supervisee Michael and supervisor Fosha about this moment.

Host: So, Michael, what was it like for you to say—not only to Diana but to all the viewers seeing the tape—that you didn't know what to do?

Supervisee: I think this is a really good example of part of why AEDP supervision is so great is because I felt secure enough with Diana to be able to take that risk and say, "Ah! I don't know what I am doing here. I don't know what is going on," right? And then I really felt met. Like I took that risk and I wanted to move right on and say like, "Help me with this technical thing," but she was like, "No. Let's talk about that," and I felt validated in that. So that felt good. And, clinically, it translates to "it is okay to not know what you are doing sometimes in session," which is going to help me regulate my anxiety and stay present with what is happening with the client. So it is like it is working on two levels.

Host: Thank you. And Diana . . . you talk about Michael's honesty and even courage and . . . Why you are doing this?

Supervisor: So that is an example of *transformance*, right, that is a risk-taking, as well as that is an action that only contributes to the integrity of the process; and that is the first thing. And the second thing is really that he takes a chance, right? And really puts himself out there by being honest about his experience. And that is really something to validate and to almost, like, take the extra step to make sure that there isn't shame about that, right? That it is not only that I don't say, "How come you don't know what you are doing?" [*laughs*] but also—"Wow—that is such an important thing to contribute!" and to acknowledge it, and there is something about making that explicit that deepens the safety and also undoes the aloneness.

Host: And I notice that you self-disclose that you share your experience—

Supervisor: Right.

Host: —as part of this, as well.

Supervisor: There's . . . he self-disclosed, and, so, towards the end of this clip that we are watching, you know, through the process that we are going through together that he settles and gets more relaxed, and something about that, you know, helps me. And I share that with him. I want to let him know that he is having an impact on me, too, and I am in this together with him. Right . . .

Now that you have some experience of us as supervisors in action, let's reflect on what you have experienced and give you the theory to satisfy your left brain and the key concepts so, moving forward together, we will have a common language. In the remainder of this chapter, we introduce seven theoretical concepts that define AEDP therapy and supervision. These concepts underlie the knowledge and capacities that are covered in the remainder of this chapter as well as the AEDP skills that are described in Chapter 2.

SEVEN KEY CONCEPTS OF AEDP

Key Concept 1: Undoing Aloneness

AEDP understands psychopathology as resulting from our unwilled and unwanted aloneness in the face of overwhelming emotional experience (Fosha, 2000b). Undoing aloneness is the first core AEDP concept. It is the therapist's goal to be with the client, and the supervisor's goal to be with the supervisee, thus undoing their aloneness in the face of whatever is hard to bear, acknowledge, or risk alone. Undoing aloneness over time, and with repeated interactions, creates secure attachment in the supervisory relationship; however, it is not a one-shot deal, and it is constantly reforged and reworked moment-to-moment, session-to-session.

We strive to undo aloneness in a number of ways. The simplest and most reliable technique is self-disclosure. When a therapist or supervisor declares, "Me, too," or, "I feel this way, too," it provides a sense that we are doing this together. We are becoming attached: collaborating and creating safety simultaneously. We aim to form an earned-secure attachment relationship in which the supervisor is explicitly helpful, emotionally engaged, and available. The attachment supervisor is a person to whom the supervisee can turn in moments of need and uncertainty: This is the sine qua non for AEDP supervision. But it is only the beginning. It is only one of many change mechanisms of AEDP's understanding of growth, change, and healing in supervisory relationships. And it is a lot: For many therapists coming to us as supervisees, this kind of relationship is new and transformative in and of itself.

Key Concept 2: Transformance/Privileging the Positive

Possibly the single most important underpinning of our supervisory and therapy sessions is the belief, supported by biology and neuroscience, that we are all self-righting organisms wired with an innate motivational tendency toward health, healing, and growth in the right environments. The AEDP word for this is *transformance*, the motivational counterpoint of resistance (Fosha, 2008, 2013b). Transformance comes to the fore in conditions of safety. Resistance, reactivity, and defensiveness arise under conditions of threat (Fosha, 2013a). As AEDP therapists and supervisors, we endeavor to cocreate safety in our sessions so that strivings for growth and change can emerge and blossom. When we actively look for what is going well, we create safety moment-to-moment in supervision and in therapy.

The *privileging of transformance*, that is, being a *transformance detective*, favors a focus on growth and change. Whenever a clinical choice presents itself, AEDP, as a rule, favors transformance over resistance; the healthy and resilient over the psychopathological; and the new, transformational, and emergent over the same old of psychopathology. We call this *privileging the positive*. The old procedural patterns, of course, need to continue to be worked with as they emerge, but hopefully and repeatedly in juxtaposition with the new and different.

Key Concept 3: Affirming, Celebrating, Delighting

AEDP supervision has an affirmative orientation. The AEDP supervisor explicitly celebrates and affirms all the supervisee is already doing successfully and also points out the leading growth edge of the work and, gently over time, what skills the supervisee needs to develop (see also the use of the AEDP Fidelity Scale, described in Chapter 4). The focus of the supervision is on the skills and achievements that are new aspects of the supervisee's repertoire and reflect his or her taking risks to put into practice new AEDP skills. Similarly, faced with a choice between focusing on an area that the supervisee has to strengthen or an area in which the supervisee is demonstrating a newfound skill or capacity, we privilege the new and emergent.

AEDP supervisors affirm, celebrate, and delight in new therapeutic achievements. We then make the most of these moments by explicitly seeking to consolidate such gains through metaprocessing the supervisee's experience of the supervisor's affirmation and delight. When we focus on transformance, we shift our attention from what's wrong to what's going well in the therapy we are supervising. We lead with affirming interventions of what we are seeing, hearing, feeling, witnessing, and experiencing. Affirmation is encouraging and confidence building, and we make it as specific as possible.

Key Concept 4: Moment-to-Moment Tracking— Making the Implicit Explicit and Specific

The fourth key concept: moment-to-moment tracking and making the implicit explicit and specific is also a skill that we will teach in Chapter 2. Simply put, moment-to-moment tracking is interpersonal mindfulness. We just notice. We do not have to know or guess how our supervisees are feeling or reacting to us—we moment-to-moment track. We take each other in with all of our senses: with our gaze, with our touch, with our hearing, with our sense of smell, with our movement and posture, with our energy and intellects. An AEDP therapist and supervisor tracks the client or supervisee moment-to-moment; she brings her awareness to the supervisee's experience by noticing physical and nonverbal communications. To get started in making the implicit explicit the AEDP supervisor gently draws the supervisee's awareness to the many ways that she is communicating: posture, movements, eye contact and facial expressions, vocal intonation, shifts, energy, and so forth, and invites her to do the same as she watches her client in the video recording. "Tracking and focusing provides a window on the state of the individual at that moment" (Fosha, 2000a, pp. 271–272), and if there is a shift or some glimmer of affect coming up in the supervisee the supervisor reflects that back. Moment-to-moment tracking is an ongoing skill. The words/interventions that help the supervisor make the implicit explicit, bringing procedural processes to the fore are short statements of our observations: "a smile," "you brighten," "mmm big sigh," "you shrug," and so forth.

Key Concept 5: Metatherapeutic Processing/Metaprocessing

Metatherapeutic processing is a key component of AEDP. It builds on and utilizes making the implicit explicit. When we put language to what we have experienced together in therapy and supervision, we are making the implicit explicit: we call this reflecting upon experience metatherapeutic processing. This is a processing of what is therapeutic about therapy or supervision. It is experientially investigating what is healing about healing. "What is usually the endpoint of the therapeutic road is [a] starting point" in AEDP (Fosha, 2000b, p. 72). A unique feature of this way of working is that change and growth are not just processes to be entrained, but experiences to be reflected upon. In AEDP, transformational experiences and change moments are explored as assiduously as traumatizing experiences: positive affects are attended to as carefully as negative ones. The standard intervention: "What is it like for you to have done this with me?" guides the supervisee to reflect on their experience, give left brain meaning to this experience, get to know explicitly and with visceral texture what the success or change is like, and do all of this in the context of the relationship with their supervisor. *Metatherapeutic processing* is the uploading of a right-brain experience into left-brain language, symbolizing and integrating it, and activating the self reflective function. It is not enough that we have experiences, we must know we have had them!

Metatherapeutic processing with a capital "M" is usually used to refer to the larger exploration of how a whole session or piece of experiential work or success has been experienced by the client or supervisee (Fosha, 2000b) while metaprocessing with a small "m" is used to refer to moment-to-moment processing of individual interventions or smaller rounds of work. *Metaprocessing* is used to describe the exploration of the supervisee's experience of an intervention or experience. We use metaprocessing to track the process itself with a supervisee. It is a key concept and a concrete activity: "How are we doing?" "What is it like to know that I, too, was an anxious supervisee?" "What was helpful about what I just said?" "What was not helpful?" "I teared up. What was that like for you?" What is usually left unsaid and implicit is made explicit and put to valuable therapeutic use through metaprocessing.

Key Concept 6: The Map of the Transformational Process— The Four States

AEDP's precision and rigor comes from its being rooted in and guided by a precisely articulated phenomenology of what the transformational process looks like as it unfolds. AEDP work is guided, moment-to-moment, by a four state transformation model (see Figure 1.1). This "map" describes what happens in the transformational process and allows AEDP supervisors to precisely know where we are and where we want to go—and applies both to the clinical material the supervisee is presenting and to the supervision session itself. Although we affirm the uniqueness of each dyad, we also know that universal wired-in emotional experiences are to be found in the phenomenology of the transformational process, which is a constant across clients and cultures.

The following four states of the transformational process apply to therapy and supervision. *State 1*, in which transformance detection occurs

AEDP: 4 STATE MAP

STATE 1 - DEFENSE / ANXIETY / DISTRESS
Defenses and defensiveness; dysregulation; anxiety; shame; closed to learning state

STATE 2 - CORE AFFECTIVE EXPERIENCES / CORE FEELINGS
Categorical emotions: joy, love, happiness, anger, sadness, fear, excitement, disgust; coordinated relational affects (feeling "in sync" with the other); corrective relational experiences; receptive affective experiences; open to learning experiences

STATE 3 - TRANSFORMATIONAL EXPERIENCES / EXPERIENCE OF CHANGE
Mastery affects of "I did it" and "I can do it!" (pride and joy); mourning the self; receptivity to feeling seen, recognized, helped, accompanied; realization affects; healing affects of gratitude, tenderness; tremulous affects associated with change for the better

STATE 4 - CORE STATE: TRUTH STATEMENTS AND A COHERENT NARRATIVE
Flow, vitality, ease, well-being, openness; closeness and intimacy; relaxation; self-empathy and empathy for others; wisdom; clarity of truth; generosity

Figure 1.1

AEDP: Four state map. Copyright © 2016 by Viktor Koen. Reprinted with permission.

along with the cocreation of safety, is characterized by defenses and inhibiting affects, and transformance phenomena. The goal is to amplify the strivings for transformance, minimize the effect of defenses, and help access more viscerally based experience. *State 2*, in which emotional and coordinated relational experiences occur, is characterized by access to core affective experiences: deep, somatically based, wired-in, core affective experience in the realms of emotion, relational experience, authentic self-experience, recognition processes, and so on, which are worked with and processed until we get a shift from a negative to a positive affective valence, and adaptive action tendencies are released. *State 3*, in which the metatherapeutic processing of transformational experience occurs, is characterized by the emergence of deep, somatically based transformational affects, invariably positive affects associated with transformational experience. *State 4*, that is, the core state, is characterized by deep, genuine, somatically based integrative and reflective experiences in which, guided by the sense of truth, therapeutic gains are consolidated.

Experience with AEDP's transformational focus has taught us that adaptive, transformational, fundamentally therapeutic experiences are accompanied moment-to-moment by somatic–affective markers, which are invariably positive. By positive, we do not necessarily mean happy but, rather, experiences that have the subjective felt sense for the client of being "right" and "true," the way being able to right a crooked picture on the wall feels right once it is properly aligned. AEDP therapists in tracking moment-to-moment fluctuations of emotional experience learn to attend to these subtle, positive somatic–affective markers that indicate that the transformational process is on track.

Key Concept 7: True Self/True Other/Responsiveness to Need in the Moment

True self, a term well known in psychodynamic therapies from the works of Winnicott (1965), refers to a subjective experience of authenticity. *True other* is an AEDP term (Fosha, 2000b, 2005) for a person's willingness to respond to the other's need in a particular moment. *True other* is not a descriptive term applied to the supervisor; it is an experiential term describing the supervisee's experience of being met and responded to by the other in a way that is just right (Fosha, 2005). A *true other* is not a perfect, idealized supervisor but one who, at meaningful moments, leans in, asks where he or she can help, gets it right—or gets it wrong and works to get it right—and then helps the supervisee reflect on it all. The supervisor is a true other to the true self of supervisee, who, in turn, can become a true other to the true self of the client. The triad becomes clear: true other–true other–true self (Prenn & Slatus, 2014).

At this point, we hope you have a sense of the feel of AEDP supervision in your right brain and the beginnings of theoretical knowledge and understanding in your left brain. Next we move into the explicit goals of AEDP supervision.

GOALS

AEDP supervisors must have a solid foundation in the stance, ethos, and principles of AEDP. They need to have not only a firm grasp of the theory and clinical application, but also specific teaching, modeling, mentorship, and supervisory skills to transmit their knowledge and expertise. The ultimate goal of supervision is to help practitioners grow, change, and translate this knowledge and these skills into their therapy sessions with their clients to achieve client growth and change.

AEDP supervisors guide clinicians' learning of AEDP in three areas:

1. knowledge: teaching theory and theoretical underpinnings;
2. capacities: experientially demonstrating the AEDP model to increase relational and emotional capacities; and
3. skills: detailing specific skills, skill sets, and intervention sequences.

These three areas go hand-in-hand, but, for the purposes of this book, we describe them separately. In the remainder of this chapter, we focus on conveying the knowledge and capacities of AEDP. We examine the skills in Chapter 2.

Knowledge

The Triangle of Experience/State 1 and State 2

Adapted from the short-term dynamic therapies and central to AEDP's maps and schemas is the triangle of experience adapted from the triangle of conflict, first introduced by Ezriel (1952) and popularized by Malan (1999). The *triangle of experience*, which has been diagrammed geometrically by AEDP faculty, teachers, and supervisors all over the world, is a triangle standing on a point (see Figure 1.2).

The triangle is easily and memorably taught at workshops by raising your arms wide in a V-shape and imagining a line drawn between your upraised hands. Imagine being the triangle of experience: Core feelings are in your chest and start there in your body, and anxiety and defense are where your hands are delineating the angles/corners of the triangle. When we avoid a core feeling or emotion (i.e., joy, love, anger, fear, disgust, surprise, happiness) or do not perceive it accurately (bottom point of the triangle = *F* for core feeling), we feel anxious (top left-hand angle = *A* for anxiety) and use defenses (top right-hand angle = *D* for defense)

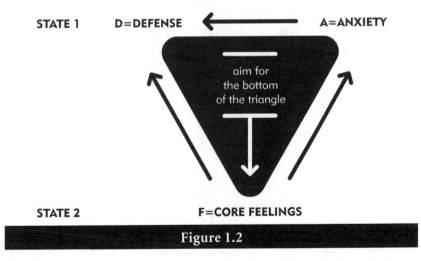

STATE 1 **D=DEFENSE** ← **A=ANXIETY**

aim for
the bottom
of the triangle

STATE 2 **F=CORE FEELINGS**

Figure 1.2

Triangle of experience. Copyright © 2016 by Viktor Koen. Reprinted with permission.

to regulate our anxiety (AEDP's State 1). At the bottom of the triangle (AEDP's State 2), in addition to core feeling or emotion, we have coordinated relational experiences, authentic self states, enjoyment, and openness (see Figure 1.3).

AEDP theory articulates that when we avoid core emotion and what we are feeling in the moment, we physically function at the top of the triangle, that is, in defenses and in anxiety and symptoms. When we are at the top of the triangle and in State 1, we are likely to be reexperiencing an old maladaptive pattern of relating to ourselves and others, whereas when we are in our bodies and in our feelings, we are in the present moment, that is, experiencing what is happening in the here-and-now. One of AEDP's goals is to safely and in a regulated way experience—with a true other—what, until now, have been feared and avoided feelings (Fosha, 2000a). AEDP's stance is to be open to emotional expression and experience (bottom of the triangle, or F, State 2) and to invite your client to join you there (Russell, 2007).

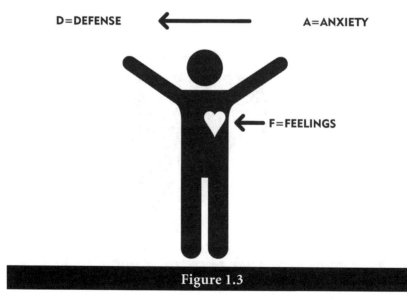

Figure 1.3

Triangle of experience: Figure with heart. Copyright © 2016 by Viktor Koen. Reprinted with permission.

In a typical supervisory hour, we will stop and draw the triangle of experience and plot onto it the client and the affect coming up in the session: What are the client's favorite defenses? How can you tell when the client is anxious? What emotions is he or she pretty comfortable with and not so comfortable with? What is the client's relational style like? What are his or her attachment strategies? Does the client tend toward a dismissive or avoidant attachment style, or is the client more preoccupied or anxious vis-à-vis the therapist and other significant relationships in his or her life? Is the client overregulated or underregulated? A typical example is demonstrated with a client who is afraid to be angry. Every time he comes forward with a statement like "I was so mad," he yawns, sighs, and lowers his head. He reports only tiredness and a wish for a vacation or break, or a day in bed. Anger is the core emotion (State 2 core affect/core feeling); his collapse, tiredness, and physical draining of energy are his defenses against the anger (top right-hand angle of the triangle, or D, State 1; see Figure 1.4). The yawning and sigh are signs that, as the client has a surge of anger, his anxiety is rising and he is trying to regulate it.

Typical defenses of an overregulated client are smiling or laughing over painful feelings; down-regulating as emotion arises; changing the

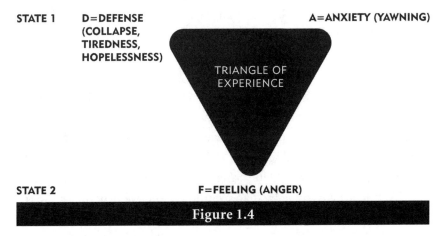

STATE 1   D=DEFENSE (COLLAPSE, TIREDNESS, HOPELESSNESS)   A=ANXIETY (YAWNING)

TRIANGLE OF EXPERIENCE

STATE 2   F=FEELING (ANGER)

Figure 1.4

Triangle map of patient anxiety, defense, and core feeling. Copyright © 2016 by Viktor Koen. Reprinted with permission.

subject; breaking eye contact; using passive voice, being vague, using generalities; intellectualizing; trying to figure things out; exhibiting self-reliance or leading with a defensive emotion such as frustration when the core feeling is sadness, hurt, or the like. Typical defenses of an under-regulated client are speeding up, weepiness and emotionality, making entreaties for help from the therapist, and focusing on another person as either the problem or the solution (see Chapter 5 for working with different attachment styles).

Typical signs of anxiety in thought and speech are preoccupation, rumination, obsession, distraction, and cognitive disruption. Signs of anxiety in the body are discomfort, jitteriness, pressured speech, restlessness, somatic complaints, intense eye contact or avoidance of eye contact, rapid breathing, perspiration, a need to use the bathroom, and so on. When our supervisees are anxious, our job as supervisors is to notice that anxiety, regulate it, normalize it, and help make space and allow the expression of feelings that are coming up from the feelings (bottom of the triangle, or F, State 2) because that is what is creating the anxiety. In therapy and in supervision, we can expect anxiety: We want to be on the lookout for it, listen for it and intuit its presence, when appropriate.

The goal is to regulate anxiety and help the client move from overuse of defenses to being increasingly able to stay with core affect/core feeling (bottom of the triangle, State 2)—in the belief that feeling one's feelings fully and knowing what we feel transforms us. Not only do we track the client in the video on the triangle of experience, but such tracking is key in supervision with our supervisees.

If a supervisee wrings her hands and says, "I'll never be able to do AEDP!" the supervisor might ask, "What just happened?" and then help plot herself on the triangle of experience. The supervisor might wonder aloud what core feeling (State 2) bubbled up inside of her that she exclaimed, "I can't do it!" (State 1: anxiety leads to defensive exclamation).

We teach the triangle by diagramming it and we experience the triangle in the video of the supervisee with his or her client. We ask supervisees, as they sit with us, where they are on the triangle. A supervisor also models where he or she is:

I noticed I became anxious when your client said she was thinking about her funeral and imagining her suicide. Then I realized I was angry at her. Now I am not anxious. Let me help you talk to her about her avoidance of her feelings and how suicidal ideation is a defense she uses against her core feelings.

And then the supervisor metaprocesses and uses his or her process as a teaching opportunity as we—supervisor and supervisee—reflect together on this sequence.

From the research of Elizabeth Schoettle (2009), we can anticipate how our supervisees feel when they are working with clients in State 1—and doing what we call State 1, top of the triangle work in which a client is functioning primarily with his or her defenses or protective strategies (i.e., D, the defense angle of the triangle). It may be helpful to think along the lines of different attachment styles and their defenses: The defensive/protective strategies of a person in State 1 who has dismissive strategies, such as intellectualization, minimization, or self-reliance, may provoke the therapist to feel pushed out, distanced, deskilled, or helpless. The anxious/preoccupied strategies of high activation and panic and anxiety may lead the therapist to feel pulled in or anxious, or may lead to problem-solving thoughts or states of feeling overwhelmed in the therapist. It is important to expect and normalize that supervisees may feel activated and as if they need to work too hard in State 1, or, equally, they may experience disengagement and feel as if they don't care (defense, State 1).

Metaprocessing and the Accompanying Affects/State 3 and State 4

Metaprocessing (State 3) started its theoretical life in AEDP as an activity, an intervention we used to reflect on experience. The standard intervention is: "What is it like to do this work with me?"

It soon became apparent that, as supervisees dropped down from defensive and anxiety-ridden functioning into either core feeling or a coordinated relational state with their supervisor, the accompanying affects were invariably pride and joy that they had succeeded (i.e., the mastery affects) and pain and sadness about other relational experiences in their past that had been unsuccessful, or not pleasurable, or not coordinated (mourning the self). In the aftermath of feeling seen, recognized, and affirmed came gratitude and feeling moved with moist eyes and tenderness (i.e., the healing affects) and surprise and delight in this new place (i.e., wow, yes affects). State 3 transformational phenomena are mastery affects: pride and joy, mourning the self, the wow and aha affects of realization, and the click of recognition and affirmation. These are often relational affects, so not only are they a part of our knowledge base, but they build capacities in our supervisees. These are invariably positive affects—even the pain of mourning the self plays back as pleasure because "having" something good has brought the sadness about what has been "not having" up until now.

In State 4, the body is relaxed and we feel clear, centered, and calm. We know the truth about our experiences, we have a coherent narrative, and no affective charge exists. We then become able to reflect on our journeys and to do so with compassion for self and even for the others who were the agents of hurt and deprivation. Often, we feel deeply connected to the universe and ourselves.

Capacities

The goal of AEDP supervision is to gradually and reliably increase proficiency and competency in AEDP. To that end, a great deal of the change work we try to bring about in our supervisory sessions involves the self of the therapist. As we work to expand relational and affective capacities, we are helping supervisees regulate their own emotional and relational experiences with us, with their clients, and with themselves.

It is here that the four state transformational process guides our work. This knowledge is how we build capacity. In AEDP supervision, as in AEDP therapy, it is by knowing how to facilitate this movement through the four states that we know how to reliably bring about change in the self of the supervisee. We actively help our supervisees move out of State 1, defense and anxiety—a closed-to-learning state—into State 2, an open-to-learning state that is accompanied by core feelings that, in supervision, are often coordinated relational states as we actively seek out corrective relational experiences (Ladany et al., 2012). When we recognize and integrate these new, positive learning, emotional, and relational experiences in the here-and-now and we metaprocess together what is new along with its historical contrast, when necessary, we build the emotional, relational capacities of our supervisees.

Other specific capacities include the ability to perceive (interpersonally) the client and (intrapsychically) themselves via moment-to-moment tracking; the ability to receive (i.e., *receptive affective capacity*) and to be affected by what is happening; and the ability to express all of this to their clients, too. AEDP therapists learn to bring ourselves—our feelings, brains, and bodies—as therapists into our therapy relationships because that is how new learning occurs. AEDP supervisors offer tentative suggestions about where supervisees need to develop clinical capacities, including experiential language interventions such that the supervisee might try to increase his or her expressive capacity.

Two additional vehicles for learning in supervision are letting the supervisee and client know the effect they are having on us emotionally. Extending from that effect is the client's or supervisee's desire to not only be known by us but to know us intellectually and emotionally in terms of our experience.

Vignette: "Have You Told Her That?"

The supervisor and supervisee have finished watching a videorecording. Both are quiet as the trajectory of healing has ended with a core state declaration of deeply felt self-compassion: "I did the best I could," the supervisee says, self-disclosing the client's effect on the therapist.

Supervisor: What do you notice inside . . . when you watch this tape and the remarkable way she stays with her pain and moves through it to more self-compassion? [**making the implicit explicit**]

Supervisee: I feel so sad for all she has suffered and so amazed at how brave she is in our sessions. Wow. She works so hard and fearlessly—and she has a lot to be afraid of inside—so much trauma.

Supervisor: Wow. You said all of that so beautifully. [**privileging the positive; affirmation**] Have you told her that?

Supervisee: No.

Supervisor: Could you tell her that? [**encouraging exploration, expanding skill set, venturing into the new**]

Supervisee: I don't know.

Supervisor: Would it be okay if I helped you? [**asking explicit permission**] [*pauses*] You put it so beautifully to me just now. What did you say? [**affirming supervisee's therapeutic competence: signaling to her "this new thing you're afraid of, you already know it"**]

Supervisee: I don't know. I think I said, "Wow."

Supervisor: Yes, you did and you said more. Let me help you find the words again. [**explicit attachment intervention: "I can be of help"**] You said you were so amazed at how brave she is.

Supervisee: Yes, I am. I could—I would say, "Lucy, I am so touched by how brave you are. I was thinking about our session together last week and I just felt so impressed by you." [**with a little prompting and help, with scaffolding, the supervisee comes up with the intervention herself**]

Supervisor: Wow. Yes, that is so lovely. [**affirmation**] Wow, look at all you did—you self-disclosed her impact on you: I am so touched. [**affirming the supervisee's intervention and exploratory ventures into new territory**] And then you let her know she exists in your heart and mind even when you are not together. [**translating what supervisee is already doing into AEDP language: basic AEDP intervention: "What seems so hard and daunting, you're already doing"**] Wow. [**expression of supervisor's delight in the supervisee**] How was it to say that out loud? [**metaprocessing the supervisee's experience of her practice of the new skill**]

Supervisee: It was good. [**positive affect associated with experiences of change for the better**]

Supervisor: Mmm hmm. Good. And how is your body feeling now? [**inviting deepening and somatic elaboration of positive experience**]

Supervisee: Better. I feel more at ease.

Supervisor: And how is it telling me? And seeing how moved I am as I see you take this huge, big risk, here with me, to say this to Lucy? [**making the implicit explicit and modeling self-disclosure of effect of supervisee on supervisor, that is, "seeing how moved I am," and metaprocessing of relational aspects of trying out a new experience**]

Supervisee: It's good. My body feels much more relaxed, yeah. More upright—like I can breathe more easily. [*pauses*] [**By asking how her body feels, the supervisor consciously seeks to create positive motivation to translate what the supervisee has just learned into action with her client.**] I think I will say this to her—I will try to say something like this to her. . . .

Supervisor: That would be great practice for you.

Supervisee: What happens if I freak her out? [**on making it real, a new question comes, as does a new anxiety**]

Supervisor: Well, what would you do after you say this to her? [**fostering the supervisee to see if she can come up with her own answer, which she does**]

Supervisee: Oh, I'd metaprocess, so I would know.

Supervisor: Yes, you'd know how she is reacting and if she is freaking out, which, by the way, I don't think she would. Then you are into another round of work—no big deal—more grist for the mill.

Notice how the supervisor modeled an experience of the very thing the supervisee was trying to learn to do. The supervisor demonstrated the trainee's impact on her as the supervisee tried to learn how to express the client's effect on her.

As we work to help our supervisees develop, we gently collect data around their different reactions to our interventions and their metaprocessing. When the supervisor asks, "How do you feel when you see how moved I am?" she is seeing if the supervisee can receive her effect on the supervisor. She may have perceived it in the supervisor's eyes, or on her face, or in her body language, but the supervisor wants to make it explicit. We will revisit moment-to-moment tracking in the Moment-to-Moment Tracking section in Chapter 2.

Expect, Notice, and Seize the New, Unusual, Unexpected, Unformulated Experience

We lean into and work explicitly with the growth potential of the supervisor–supervisee relationship. And when we see moments to slow down and have a new experience together, we mine them for their transformational properties. This focus on and metaprocessing of the new, novel, and unexpected is where growth occurs in our relational and intrapsychic capacities. It is in areas of newness and novelty, specifically in experiences that go against our procedural knowledge, that growth and change occur. When we ask, "What is it like to have this experience with me right now?" we ask our supervisees to know that they are having a new, different experience with us. We know the territory of this unformulated experiential landscape: We know to expect that, as we lay down new neural networks, supervisees often say, "This is weird." Then, as they formulate their experience, they say, "I don't know how to put it into words." And then they are able to articulate what it is not—the absence of something. This is before they say precisely what it is. So, "It is not fear or anxiety or dysregulation! It is the absence of what I usually feel. It is excitement, or maybe . . . eagerness."

In this next case example, a new supervisee comes in for an AEDP supervision meeting. She answers a direct question about how she feels coming in for her first meeting with her supervisor (i.e., Prenn). Note how the supervisor wants to make the relational contact with her explicit and what happens when they metaprocess the supervisor's attempt.

Vignette: New Experience "This Is Weird"

Supervisor: How do you feel coming in for your first meeting with me?

Supervisee: Oh, I am all over the place. I think I am coming down with something. I almost canceled. I have a client at the clinic where I work . . .

he needs an extra session . . . I said no. Now he is texting me. I should have met with him, it would have been easier; but I am not feeling well.

Supervisor: Oh, my. I am so glad you are telling me. So can we just check in? This is our first meeting; you are not feeling well healthwise, and I wonder if it is okay to ask how are you feeling emotionally meeting with me?

Supervisee: Is this therapy or supervision?

Supervisor: It is supervision. You are having a reaction to my checking in with you?

Supervisee: Yes. I guess I am not used to someone checking in with me. I mean, I do when I am the therapist, of course I do, but not on this side.

Supervisor: Right. So, is it okay to ask you this? How is it with you that I am asking? [**explicit asking permission**]

Supervisee: Oh, it's nice. It's—I don't know—weird.

Supervisor: Say more. . . .

Supervisee: Yes. A part of me feels relaxed and a part of me isn't sure I am going to like you focusing on our relationship. I am not used to that being a part of supervision. I think I just want to show my tapes and learn AEDP!

Supervisor: Right. I get that. And in my experience the best way to learn AEDP and keep our supervision on track is through tending to the relationship together so that we can keep it feeling safe enough to do this work together.

Supervisee: Okay, I get that.

Supervisor: And again [*says in gentle, slow voice*]. How is it? How are we? How is it for you to be with me?

Supervisee: [*wrinkles her brow*]

Supervisor: Your forehead is wrinkling. [**notice nonevaluative, for example, "frowning"; just descriptive**]

Supervisee: I wasn't expecting this.

Supervisor: So how is it in this moment?

Supervisee: "Weird, new, different." [**Notice her words.**]

Supervisor: Yes, weird, new, different. I love those words. They often—and I hope it is okay to step back and reflect for a moment and use this as a teaching point—words like "I am not used to this" often signal that we are creating a new experience together. That is exciting for me to notice. How is it for you to know my take on this? [**metaprocess**]

Supervisee: Oh, I think I get it. Right. I remember that from your workshop. You showed a recording of that young man. He says that—what did he say, "I am just not used to . . . I don't expect it."

Supervisor: Yes, that is exactly what he says. How good you remember that . . . And is it okay with you if we stay with you for just another moment—how is it for you to be getting it? [**asking permission; time limit; metaprocessing**]

Supervisee: Good, phew, relief. Yes, good!

AEDP supervision is experiential and relational. It tends to the relationship explicitly. We end the session with a metatherapeutic intervention: "How was this meeting for you today?"

The Teach/Treat Line

Everything we do or don't do as supervisors is modeling how to work as a therapist. It is supervision and not therapy; however, we are therapists in a supervisory role. We are reliable, predictable, and dependable. We meet promptly at the appointed time. If we are running late or must change an appointment time, we check in and apologize, as we would with a client. We explicitly offer help and seek to be available.

A central task in AEDP supervision is to develop supervisees' clinical capacities to treat their clients. This initially agreed on mandate that is recontracted again and again gives the supervisor explicit latitude to ask permission to work directly with emotion, experience, defenses, attachment style, and anxiety in the here-and-now of the supervisory relationship. The AEDP supervisor does so while explicitly respecting that this is supervision in the service of the client; it is not therapy. The process-oriented nature of AEDP supervision means that one can gently work around what is happening with a supervisee who is in a triggered, activated, or defensive moment without inquiring or needing to know the specific historic details of the dynamics. This is a common experience in AEDP supervision. A supervisee might say, "Oh, this again . . . I know exactly where this comes from!" The supervisor might gently inquire if it would be productive to stay with the experience of what is happening and to process emotion to completion without ever knowing or needing to know "where this comes from."

Treatment Moments/Teaching Point

The American Psychological Association's (APA) *Ethical Principles of Psychologists and Code of Conduct* (APA, 2010) state clearly that treatment in supervision is not an ethical breach of any kind as long as it is in the service of the client and as long as it is agreed to by both supervisor and supervisee. The AEDP techniques of making the implicit explicit and asking permission mean that contracting around a treatment moment occurring in supervision can be made explicit. It is common for a supervisee to struggle personally with the things they want to learn as therapists. For example, is a supervisee able to take in a compliment and feel proud of him- or herself (i.e., receptive affective capacity)? It is at this juncture—the teach/treat line—that expansion of the self of the therapist–supervisee often takes place. Current affective neuroscience supports this experiential way of working in supervision: Implicit, procedural memory and our internal working models change through access to the limbic system, where new learning and memory reconsolidation occurs (Badenoch, 2008; Ecker, Ticic, & Hulley, 2012).

We can use a moment of treatment or a round of work as a teaching point. We go through a round of work together, meaning that we start with a focus or an entry point (see Chapter 2) and then explore it together. We then can use that entry point as a teaching point: This is real and it is our experience together. We might say, "Would it be all right with you if we went back over all we just experienced together and looked at it together as a teaching point?" The supervisee has a treatment moment, reflects on the experience, and the supervisor teaches from what has just happened explicitly.

Teach/Treat Vignette: "That's Enough Now"

The supervisee and therapist (i.e., Prenn) are watching the first minutes of a recorded session with a client who has broken out of old patterns during the course of the week. "I didn't take it personally," the client says. "I thought I did a very good job at the interview. They liked me and hired me, and now they have a hiring freeze. They said they will circle around to me and hire me when the freeze ends. I trust that they will. I didn't attack myself. It wasn't personal. I knew that, and I didn't take it personally at all."

"That's fantastic," the therapist says. The client smiles and her eyes light up. The therapist continues, "Look at the difference. You sat up straighter, smiled, and told me, 'I didn't take it personally.'"

They smile at each other for a millisecond, and then the client's smile fades, her eyes seem to lose their focus, and she looks away.

"I still get scared," she says.

"I know," the therapist says.

The client talks for about 4 minutes about how she used to feel scared. The therapist–supervisee, who is accustomed to exploring the ways we feel bad, nods and listens. Then the therapist returns to what she has chosen as an entry point of this round of work: a metaprocessing and cementing of the experience of doing something different. She says, "Would it be okay to go back—how is it to do something so different and have us reflect on it together?"

"It is good." Again, a tiny fleeting smile, and therapist smiles, too. The therapist says, "Your students love you." She names two or three things that are positive about the client.

The client smiles tentatively and tries to stay with therapist. She says, "Yes, I have the heart, but I don't have the brains. I am not like the other professors." She goes on to describe all the ways she is not smart like her counterparts at the university. The therapist listens and nods, and explores how inadequate she has felt in the past. She does not stay with the positive.

"Wait. I . . .," the supervisor blurts out. "Can I stop the tape here? Doesn't she have a PhD?" We stop the tape and talk.

"Yes," the therapist–supervisee says. "Yes." [*Both laugh.*]

"This is so funny," the supervisee says. "I had the feeling—ack—anxiety—and the thought—'that's enough now.'"

"Oh, yes . . . Tell me," the supervisor says.

"I could have kept going. Huh, I see that so clearly now."

"Let's watch it again," the supervisor suggests.

They watch 2 minutes again and then talk. "Wow," says the supervisee, "I am afraid if we are too positive, my client will leave."

"Wow," the supervisor replies.

"And," the supervisee continues, "we were five kids—we had to give to ourselves. I am learning this now." She starts to pack up.

"Oh, wait. We have time," the supervisor says. "We still have almost 10 minutes."

"Oh," she says. "I had that feeling again and I thought, 'That's enough now.'"

"Would it be okay if we stayed with it?" the supervisor asks. [**asking permission**]

At the end of our meeting, the supervisee and supervisor say good-bye. We have time to spare, and the clock is in line of sight of us both. "All right then," the supervisee says, as she almost pushes past the supervisor to leave. "Could we? Would it be okay if we just spent a moment?" [**asking permission**]

The supervisee says, "Argh, I am having that feeling again: 'That's enough now.'"

"Your allotment," says the supervisor, making a gesture of cupping her hands together. "There were five of you when you were a child and only this much for you."

"Yes! My allotment," says the supervisee.

"Can we stretch that a millisecond?" The supervisor moves her cupped hands apart.

They both laugh, and the supervisee stops and tries to stay another moment with the supervisor. "This is hard to do," she says.

"I know," says the supervisor. "That is why we are doing it for just a few more seconds here, now. I know it's hard. And what's it like now?"

"Uncomfortable and good!" she says. They make eye contact and laugh.

This is an example not only of a treatment moment in supervision overlapping a teaching point but also of a parallel process. It is the uncanny nature of resonance, right-brain to right-brain communication, and the work of mirror neurons that our supervisees' growing edge of receptive capacity, for example, is almost exactly the same as the capacity that they are helping their clients grow into. *Receptive capacity* is the ability to receive whatever we offer to our supervisees. It is expanded by staying with it and trying to stretch it with the supervisee.

CONCLUSION

This chapter started with two transcripts of AEDP supervision in action. We emphasized the importance of positive relational experiences to encourage risk-taking and dopamine-rich, open-to-learning states. Then we introduced the seven key concepts of AEDP: (a) undoing aloneness; (b) transformance and privileging the positive; (c) affirming, celebrating, and delighting; (d) moment-to-moment tracking, making the implicit explicit and specific; (e) Metatherapeutic processing–metaprocessing; (f) the four-state map of the transformational process; and (g) true self/ true other/responsiveness to need in the moment. We explained the triangle of experience and how to use it in supervision. The chapter concluded with how to use treatment moments as teaching opportunities and how to notice and seize new, unexpected experiences for the growth of our supervisees. Chapter 2 translates these concepts into practical skills.

2

Essential Skills

This chapter outlines the skills we use to translate theory into clinical practice. We start with the role of the relationship and the stance of the supervisor in the relationship. Then we guide you through what we teach and how we teach it—including the essential skills of accelerated experiential dynamic psychotherapy (AEDP) and the language of interventions—highlighting experiential techniques imported directly into supervision from AEDP.

THE ROLE OF THE RELATIONSHIP IS CENTRAL

Although it has been widely acknowledged that the relationship is crucial to supervision (Angus & Kagan, 2007; Budge & Wampold, 2015; Ellis & Ladany, 1997; Watkins, 2012; Watkins, Budge, & Callahan, 2015; Watkins &

http://dx.doi.org/10.1037/00000016-003
Supervision Essentials for Accelerated Experiential Dynamic Psychotherapy, by N. C. N. Prenn and D. Fosha

Milne, 2014), what is unique to AEDP therapy and supervision is how we work with relational experience. We make the experience of the relationship and relatedness explicit, and then we work with that experience both experientially (i.e., procedural knowledge) and reflectively (i.e., declarative knowledge; Binder, 1993; Watkins, 2012). The use of the relationship is a particular skill set that we explicitly teach (Levenson, 1995). "What is your reaction to me right now?" "How are you experiencing me now?" "What is your sense of me right now?" These are interventions that work well. One of AEDP's major contributions to psychotherapy is unpacking the different ways in which we explicitly use the therapist's— or the supervisor's—self and experience.

Theoretically, the relationship is a vehicle for change (Lipton & Fosha, 2011); experientially, we as supervisors use the in vivo lived history of our supervisor–supervisee real relationship to facilitate change. The relationship is layered: supervisor and supervisee, therapist and client, and then, also through the work, the relationship that develops between supervisor and client. In supervision that is going well, all three individuals—client, therapist, and supervisor—are in relationship, and through that relationship are learning and changing, and are in transition. As a senior clinician new to AEDP said,

> All my training up until now was about how to take myself out of the room and out of the relationship. And now neuroscience and attachment theory is saying it is the relationship that is central to healing. I know that is right, I want to do it, and I don't know how to do it.

How to Be: I Interact; Therefore, I Am (Tronick, 1998)

The supervisor's drive to connect, his or her ability to be responsive to need in each moment, and the supervisor's fund of AEDP knowledge, expertise, and experience combine to make him or her a good enough supervisor (channeling Winnicott's, 1960, good enough mother for her supervisee). When supervisor and supervisee show up authentically, and the supervisee takes the risk to ask for something he or she needs and the supervisor responds to that need—responsiveness to need in the moment—we describe this as *true self–true other relating* (Fosha, 2000b, 2005). The supervisor is a true other to the true self of the supervisee, who, in turn, is a true other to the true self of his or her client (Prenn & Slatus, 2014; see Figure 2.1 concept by Jessica Slatus).

These experiences of true self–true other relating that are lived through together by supervisee and supervisor are cocreated; they increase safety and security, and result in further exploration and risk-taking. The attachment relationship, the secure base (Bowlby, 1988), is continually checked in on and renewed through lived-together moments in which we show up and try to be of help again and again. If we were to translate into words the felt sense of security that emerges in this relationship, they might be:

> I can be emotionally real with my supervisor and she will help me. She will understand me and normalize my struggles, and together we will track what I do and what needs to be done. She will point out what is going well and add some of her own ideas, as well, so I can expand my sense of self as a therapist.

AEDP therapy aims to be a transformational therapy. AEDP supervision, being first and foremost experiential, aims to be a transformational supervision. Eileen Russell (2015) has referenced the work of

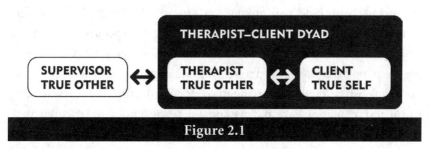

THE ROLE OF THE SUPERVISOR
SUPERVISOR AS TRUE OTHER TO THE THERAPIST–CLIENT DYAD

Figure 2.1

Role of the supervisor as true other–true self. Copyright © 2016 by Viktor Koen. Reprinted with permission.

psychoanalyst Christopher Bollas (1987), who talked about the mother's being a transformational other to the baby's transforming self or self-in-transition. Russell, channeling Bollas, talked about the therapist as transformational other to the client's self-in-transition. Here, we are extending that terminology to the supervisory process: The supervisor is transformational other to the supervisee's transitional self in the context of the supervision he or she is conducting in which the supervisee, in turn, is transformational other to the client's self-in-transition. Thus, in AEDP, we have the triad of the transformational other (i.e., supervisor) to self-in-transition/transformational other (i.e., supervisee/therapist) to self-in-transition (i.e., client).

"The ideal supervisor ... exhibits high levels of empathy, understanding, unconditional positive regard, flexibility, concern, attention, investment, curiosity, and openness" (Carifio & Hess, 1987, p. 244). Frequently, these seem to be personal characteristics: Supervisors are born and not made. Yet, woven into the theory of AEDP are a stance and relational skills that inform how to "be" and delineate how to "do" all of the above. The AEDP framework supports the clinician's ability to not only learn skills but cultivate these capacities. We can do specific behaviors to be this way and we can say particular things to express these characteristics.

The AEDP Supervisory Stance

A number of discrete behaviors double as personality traits, yet they are teachable via the AEDP stance and technique (Fosha, 2008). These behaviors include being kind, real, present, and generous (Pizer, 2012); being with; fostering positively toned interactions; and cocreating positive interactions and repairing stressful, negatively toned interactions (Schore, 2001). Teaching them means going beyond mirroring and engaging in dyadic affect regulation (Fosha, 2000b), behaving in oxytocin-engendering ways, making use of and regulating gaze and eye contact, being tender and owning up to lapses in sincerity (Ferenczi, 1933), and fostering the client's sense that he or she exists in your heart and mind (Fosha, 2000b, adapted from Fonagy, Steele, Steele, Moran, & Higgitt, 1991).

The supervisor models the AEDP therapeutic stance by welcoming the supervisee; taking delight in specifics about the supervisee; and affirming, validating, and appreciating everything that the supervisee is doing well already. Just like the AEDP therapist, the AEDP supervisor is welcoming, affirming, validating, self-disclosing, delighting, celebrating, collaborative, vulnerable, open (not defensive), and responsive. Most of all, he or she wants to genuinely relate and help.

THE SKILLS

Some concepts are easily translated into specific techniques or technical skills to teach you what to do and say to be the kind of supervisor that the AEDP supervisor aims to be. Here, we include the language of actual interventions so you can put into practice the skills we are talking about. You also can see how each concept can be broken down into user-friendly techniques that you can easily incorporate into a supervisory session. We divide these skills into five categories: experiential, privileging the positive, relational, affective/emotional, and integrative/reflective.

1. Experiential Skills

Slowing Down

Slowing down is the foundational skill in experiential work. Supervisees must slow down to learn to know their internal experience. Phrases to start this process are: "Let's slow this down," "let's take a breath here," "we have time," "let's pause here," "mmm ... a lot here," "let's go back," "let's stay here," "let's stay with this," and "can we ...?" The supervisor is saying explicitly and implicitly that he or she knows how to help: "I know the pace is too fast" or "let's slow down." The supervisor knows what to do; he or she actively helps and wants to help. Statements often are more effective than questions. Nonverbal behaviors work equally well here: We take a breath ourselves and exhale, we slow down our speech, and we make a slow-down gesture with our hands or breathe deliberately.

Experiential Language

We try to use experiential language with our supervisees and teach them how to use this language with their clients. We use experiential language when we are working to shift from the top of the triangle, State 1, to the bottom, State 2—from prefrontal cortical thinking to limbic experience (see Figure 1.2). We have more than one tone of voice in supervision and therapy: We have our everyday, social, top-of-the-triangle tone of voice and the more dropped-down voice that comes with emotion and emotional state-sharing in session (Schore, 2001, 2009). A part of the experiential use of language is in the tone, pace, pitch, and prosody of our speech: We try to slow down our speech and lower our tone, which tends to come from an internal relaxation on the part of the supervisor. The use of experiential language is to help clients and supervisees make the shift from left-brain thinking to the right-brain embodied feeling. We try to use short, monosyllabic words, when possible; we try for one intervention at a time; we try to use Germanic everyday words like *fall* rather than Greco-Roman words like *autumn*, *belly* rather than *stomach*, and *important* rather than *interesting*. Some interventions work better than others to facilitate and deepen attachment relationships. Monosyllables like *huge*, *wow*, and *this is big* work well. Vagueness on the part of the supervisor to his or her supervisee and, in turn, therapist to client, makes space for their experience: "something's coming up here" and "a lot here . . ." are multipurpose phrases that work well.

Languaging Interventions

We have said that we want to make the attachment relationship explicit, and so we need to adjust the experiential attachment language with closeness and relatedness, according to the comfort level of our supervisees. For some supervisees, the language of *we* is initially too intimate. Notice the difference between the abstract and less personal "*this* is moving" to the more personal "*I* feel moved by *you*." When we take the first and second person pronouns *you* and *I* and *we* and *us* out of our interventions, we lower the heat of the relational thermostat. When we put them in, we up the relational ante, making it more explicit and more experiential. How we language our interventions is critical. Again, notice the difference between the explicit attachment language in "we are working on this together" or "let's work on this together" and the more distancing "these are the stated goals of this supervision."

Moment-to-Moment Tracking

This is a multifaceted skill. It is the microtracking, the zoom-in-tight focus into the here-and-now experience of the supervisee with supervisor. What kinds of things are we tracking? Posture, movement, tension, relaxation, facial expression, shifts in eye contact, speech, tone, volume, pace, coherence, breathing, and so forth. AEDP's skill-building involves the sequencing of interventions and breaking down AEDP into one achievable skill at a time. A beginning AEDP therapist who has been taught to pay attention to the words, figure things out, and interpret may well be daunted by the idea of using what is called *moment-to-moment tracking*. So we break it down and suggest that, for 1 week, the beginning therapist will track body movement only. When we divide a learning task into component pieces, it becomes more manageable. "How about you try once or twice in every session to notice the hands, arms, legs, and feet of your client; notice shifts, movement. Let's practice your observational, perceptive skills this week. Just that." This becomes "homework" for our supervisees to practice week to week.

Next, we build the skill of how to intervene through expressive skills. The supervisor tells the supervisee,

> Let's try to notice in words how to express to your client what we see. Let's start with statements and not questions. For example, "your foot is telling a story"; "your foot had a reaction to that"; "your foot is moving"; "wow, your foot and now my foot—a lot of energy as we are talking."

Learning to pepper a session with moment-to-moment tracking statements is a good way to get started in experiential body-based psychotherapy. It is a way of quietly and unobtrusively saying, "I notice." It is an indirect self-disclosure: I am the kind of person who notices. We notice nonverbal behaviors. For example, "you made a fist"; "your hands are talking"; "expressive hands today" (the supervisor might make the same movements); "I am moving around a lot, too, I notice"; and "hmm . . . I wonder what your hands are saying." And then we are off to the relationship races: "How is it to know I notice, to get a sense of my gently noticing you?" Whenever possible, we use the *two-step intervention*: a "noticing" and its metaprocessing.

Next, we teach questions that ask more of a client because they ask for a response: "What is your foot saying?" "Don't stop: It is talking! It is helping us." "If we held a microphone to your foot (and you didn't think) and you just spoke, I wonder what the first words from your foot would be?" These are ways to build skills in supervision.

Most supervisees will come in week after week having tried out a specific skill, and if they have been successful, we build on that success and keep adding skills. If they have noticed that they are unable to practice a skill, we get curious together about what happens for them. We practice in the here-and-now of the supervision session with our supervisees. We unobtrusively moment-to-moment track their nonverbal communication and we make what we notice explicit: "You smile! You brighten." "Your brow is furrowing . . . something there." In this way, during a session, we can give the supervisee an experience of being on the receiving end of a skill.

Making the Implicit Explicit and Specific, and the Explicit Experiential

When we make the implicit explicit, we shine a light on what is happening specifically and in detail experientially. We do not let the procedural hum of all of this live in the background of our work: We bring it to the foreground. It is this making the implicit explicit that brings the work into the here-and-now and allows for the possibility of a new experience. We want to notice our supervisee's patterns of relating to him- or herself and to us, and by bringing our focus to what it is like together in this moment, we model the workings of AEDP therapy. We ask for details from our supervisees and teach them to ask for details from their clients. It is in the specific example and the details of an experience that the procedural ways of interacting come to the fore.

Entry Points

When we slow down and moment-to-moment track, we make use of what we are tracking to find places to enter, to intervene. We call these *entry points*. When we notice a shift or a glimmer of something affective or relational emerging internally or between us, it is a moment we want to notice and seize (Frederick, 2005), and so we stop the supervisee. It is important to seize it, to identify it, mark it, discuss it, imprint it. The supervisee did something and it really worked. It is an important moment because it is a moment when a change involving a state shift has occurred. We want to notice, seize, stay, and understand what happened and why, and help make it happen many more times. At such moments, it is important to stop the action to process and metaprocess.

Asking Permission

It is a general rule of experiential therapies to ask open-ended questions and avoid questions that invite a simple yes or no answer. This is true in AEDP except when we use the most crucial intervention: asking permission. "Is it okay with you?" "Can we . . . together?" "Would it be all right if we stay with this/if we look at this together?" We want to emphasize this intervention is critical to promote safety, and that we want a strong, "Yes" or head nod indicating "Yes!" before we proceed. Probably the biggest mistake we see in therapists new to AEDP is not asking permission frequently enough. A way to invite a "No" and give permission to say "No" is to follow up with the words, "Would you feel comfortable enough with me to say, 'No!'" or "You can say 'No'—you know."

Using Phenomenology: The Schemas of AEDP Anchor the Work

We use the phenomenology of experience to guide us. The triangle of experience and the four states of the transformational process (see Figures 1.1 and 1.2) are the central schematics of all our work. What skills accompany them in supervision? Together with our supervisees, we draw triangles to map their clients' defenses, anxiety, and feelings, and we use the four states to describe what we are seeing. We ask our supervisees, "Where are we on the triangle? What state is your client in?" The aim is almost always to be moving down through the four states, from the top of the triangle, State 1; to the bottom, State 2; to the transformational affects, State 3; until we reach the integrative consolidation of State 4.

The Interruption. In AEDP, we announce our subjectivity by saying, "I am thinking," "I am feeling," "This is what occurs to me," and so forth. We announce our ability to play with supervisory interventions by starting to say something and course-correcting as we speak:

> This is what I am seeing and feeling as I watch your client . . . Wait . . . Let me check in with myself. That doesn't seem quite right. Would it be okay if I paused for a moment? As I am saying this, I notice I am having another reaction inside of me.

The course correction spoken out loud of our internal experience—"As I say this, this doesn't seem quite right"—is a technique we call the *interruption.* Interrupting yourself as a supervisor is useful both because it allows you to think aloud and to model that it's important not to be too wed to any one idea. In addition, this technique is useful in therapy when we start to say something and realize it doesn't seem quite right (Bollas, 1987), or a client is showing signs of emotion that need attending to in the moment.

The Completion, a.k.a. "Finish That . . ." Finish the sentence. When emotion, vulnerability, anxiety is present, we are more likely to cognitively disrupt: Supervisees and clients start a sentence and stop. This is a moment to use the completion. We ask the supervisee or client to finish the sentence; for example, "I am afraid . . .," "Finish that . . .," "I am afraid she is going to be angry with me," and "Tell me more."

Contain With a Time Limit. When we ask permission, we often use a time limit to give a structure and to contain a piece of work. "Would it be okay if we stayed with this together for 5 minutes?"

2. Privileging the Positive

Explore, Expand, and Harness Excitement, Enjoyment, and Success

Under the umbrella of privileging the positive is AEDP's aim to explore, expand, and explicitly enjoy positively attuned and positively valenced interactions. When we have disruptions or negatively valenced interactions, we seek to repair immediately and assiduously until we reestablish a synchronized state that feels good. Learning a new way of working is difficult, but we head into what is hard together and focus on the positive affects of curiosity, excitement, and success that emerge. We know that we need to harness these positive affects, know how to harness them, and know their function in improved memory, flexibility, and creativity (Fosha, 2007, 2009a; Russell, 2015, p. 100, pp. 265–270; Russell & Fosha, 2008).

Welcoming, Affirming, Validating, Delighting, Celebrating

Above all else, affirming and supporting explicitly and specifically all that a supervisee is clearly doing well translates into confidence building in supervision. It says, "You are already doing this—keep doing it and do more of it!"

Michael Glavin, the trainee whose supervision session is documented in the American Psychological Association DVD *Accelerated Experiential Dynamic Psychotherapy (AEDP) Supervision* (Fosha, 2016; see https://www.apa.org/pubs/videos/4310958.aspx), said that his previous, non-AEDP experience of supervision had been much more focused on things that he was doing wrong. A supervisor who is experienced and has much clinical wisdom to impart can unwittingly shame a supervisee who is, by his or her very position, less experienced and seeking help and guidance (Sarnat, 2016).

3. Relational Skills

Attachment: The "We-ness" of Attachment

Under the umbrella term of *attachment* are specific relational techniques to translate attachment theory into clinical practice, including undoing aloneness, which is a key AEDP concept and an actionable behavior. Typical statements and questions used in these interventions include: "Can *we* look at this *together*?" "*I am here* and listening ... Tell me more ...," "Would it be okay if *we* paused here/rewound the tape here?" "Where are *we* right now, *you and I*?" and "This is such a difficult moment." Meanwhile, body language makes our presence implicit and explicit by nodding and leaning forward to make obvious that we are concentrating.

The notion of existing in each other's heart and mind can be turned into an actionable behavior by remembering the supervisee's history and clients, and making this explicit. You might say to your supervisee, "I remember your client: I have seen Martha [or Jimmy or Rob] before. Of course, I remember." Or, "I remember what you were practicing last week. Did you practice the interventions? How did that go with Linda? Let's take a look at Jack this week, and do tell me in three sentences how the interventions with Linda went!"

The supervisee is strongly encouraged to articulate what he or she is experiencing in the supervisory session and how it makes him or her feel. The supervisee's experience of the supervisor and that person's supervising are an essential part of constructing a two-way relationship in which both parties feel seen, heard, and felt. The supervisee must feel helped and supported in the relationship. Invitations from the supervisor to compare views are crucial: "This is how I see it," you might say, "but what's your take on this?" (Fosha & Slowiaczek, 1997, p. 239).

Self-Disclosure

Self-disclosure often makes therapists nervous, whether in therapy or supervision. The idea that there is a correct, "neutral" way of working looms large. It is helpful to define and be clear about what we mean by *self-disclosure* and how and why we use it.

There are two main kinds of self-disclosure. The first, *self-experiencing self-disclosure*, happens when the supervisor describes his or her own affect and process as it unfolds in the session and from session to session. In many ways, our interactions reveal us: When we notice sadness, for instance, we reveal that we are the kind of person who notices and feels comfortable noticing and talking about sadness. If we are silent when difficult feelings come up, we are revealing just as much, but different, information, "for absence has presence" (Wachtel, 1997, p. 245). Consider a technique that Greenberg and Watson (2005) called "saying all of it" (p. 128): It is not enough to say we feel angry, delighted, or distanced by a supervisee; we need to say all of it and tell the supervisee the specifics, what the content is, and what our process is. We thereby make the implicit explicit and specific. Interventions that demonstrate this idea include language like "I feel you . . . move away, relax, come forward, shift, tense up" and "I felt that . . . something shifted."

The quickest way to deepen experience between two people is when one of them says something personal, particularly something affect laden (Prenn, 2009). *Self-revealing self-disclosure* happens when the supervisor describes actual life experiences, triumphs, vulnerabilities, uncertainties, and dilemmas. Self-disclosure is a secure attachment-creating intervention. The intervention typically begins with language like "I have felt that too . . ."; "I know that personally . . ."; or "our histories are different, and I, too, know how it feels to feel disappointed/scared/humiliated. . . ." The supervisor might self-disclose about the supervisee's effect on him or her, by saying, "I thought about you this week: I got stuck in a similar place with a similar client, and my conversation with you the week before helped me get unstuck more quickly." In working with the client, the supervisee might say, "I am moved by your . . .," "I appreciate, wow, I am touched by how you . . ."

Revealing vulnerability is key. Say a supervisee is lamenting that a client is leaving her practice. She is wondering why he might have left. A supervisor might lean in and say that she, too, has had a client leave after two sessions and add that she really doesn't know why. The supervisor says, "I have lots of ideas and, ultimately, I don't know why he left." Then she might ask, "How is this to hear that I know this, too—clients sometimes leave after one, two, or 10 sessions and we don't always know why? What is that like to know?" We are in rich, mutative territory when the supervisor communicates that she is imperfect, she makes mistakes, she doesn't know things, and she is vulnerable. She doesn't work perfectly with every client who walks through her door.

Supervisors can use metaprocessing to inquire into many facets of our supervisees' experience regarding self-disclosure. Some of these interventions can be characterized as metacognitive: "What is it like to think that thought?" "How is it for you to think: 'I did self-disclose and metaprocess with my client?'" "What is it like to go from thinking you can't do AEDP to noticing all the ways you are already doing AEDP!" Other interventions are meta-affective: "What is it like to feel the gratitude you just described?" "How is this feeling of self-compassion sitting with you?" "What is it like to feel sad for your client when you said you felt numb before?" Still other interventions are metasomatic: "What is it like to sit taller in your seat?" "What is it like to sense the strength in your arms?" "How is it for you to sense these changes inside right now?" And others are metatherapeutic: "How does taking in my care and support sit with you?" "How is it for you to sense our connection?" "What is it like to have done this work with me today?" We can also describe these inquiries as "What's it like?" questions, "What are you noticing?" questions, and "How is it going for us?" questions (Lipton, 2013).

4. Affective/Emotion-Focused Techniques

Shifting From Reflective Listening to Experiential Exploring

Experiential–dynamic work is a way of working that makes a shift from reflective listening and response to experiential exploration. A first skill we teach in AEDP is noticing an affect-laden word or an emotion-rich word and exploring its internal experience. An *affect-laden word* is one that is alive with emotion, such as *sad, disappointed, remorseful, heartbroken,* or *frustrated*. For instance, in the supervision session that is on the DVD (Fosha, 2016) accompanying this book and is discussed in detail in Chapter 3, the supervisor notices and seizes "squirmy" as the affect-laden word that becomes the entry point to a rich and productive exploration. Any word that describes an experience and has oomph or energy, or a notable lack thereof, becomes a focus of our exploration. The most obvious way of intervening—which therapists trained in other treatment modalities use and that is learned in graduate school—is reflective responding and explaining instead of exploring. In AEDP, we believe that clients will be helped most by knowing what they are experiencing and how they are experiencing it. This essential skill is the shift from reflective responding to experiential working.

Compare these two short examples. First:

Client: I feel so sad.

Supervisee: It sounds like you feel sad.

Client: Yes I do. It seems hopeless.

Supervisee: It seems hopeless right now.

We call this kind of back-and-forth *ping-pong*: We give the emotion back to the client or supervisee.

On the other hand, consider this example (see Figure 2.2):

Client: I feel so sad.

Therapist: What is that like—that sadness?

Client: Ugh. It seems hopeless.

Therapist: And that hopeless feeling . . . What is that like?

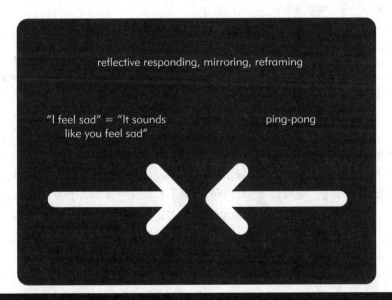

Figure 2.2

Ping-pong reflective responding, mirroring, and reframing. Copyright © 2016 by Viktor Koen. Reprinted with permission.

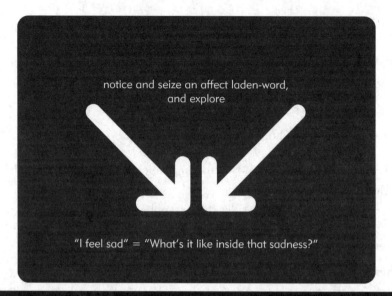

Figure 2.3

Notice and seize an affect-laden word. Copyright © 2016 by Viktor Koen. Reprinted with permission.

Client: It feels like a weight.

Therapist: That is great you notice that. Where is that weight inside your body? (See Figure 2.3.)

When we teach this skill, we tell the supervisee about it: For every affect-laden word you notice, try to notice and seize the word, and explore what it is like. The supervisor might model this skill first and give the practicing of the skill for unofficial homework so that the supervisee has the experience of the skill and the didactic learning, too.

Modeling the Intervention

Supervisor: How does it feel to imagine doing this?

Supervisee: It feels a little daunting.

Supervisor: And that daunting feeling—What is that like inside of you? Is it okay to ask?

Supervisee: Yes, it's okay to ask. Ya . . . I can feel myself shrink inside.

Supervisor: Is it okay to stay with that? What is the shrinking like inside?

Supervisee: A fluttery sensation inside my chest—right here [*puts her hand to her collarbone*] and the thought comes that I won't be able to. And then the fear that I won't be any good at AEDP, and you won't like me.

Supervisor: Right, okay. And how is it to let me know that?

Supervisee: It feels vulnerable.

Supervisor: And how is that for you to feel vulnerable with me?

Portrayal

A *portrayal* is a specific technique used to build emotional and expressive capacities, and to mine the dynamics of a particular relationship in AEDP therapy and supervision. Portrayals can be real or imagined scenes from the past, present, or future in which the client or supervisee is invited to have a reparative, or a feared, avoided, or a wished-for experience through the vehicle of imagination. The more vivid and specific the imagery, the more connections there are to dynamic and affective experiencing. The imagery and metaphor of portrayals activate almost as many areas of the brain as actual lived experience (Pally, 2000, pp. 33, 132). Portrayal experiences in session assist in the processing of dynamic material and can help to bring countertransference issues to light. The language of portrayals expands the supervisee's experiential, emotional repertoire. As supervisees gradually face—intrapsychically—people, affects, and situations they previously avoided because of their painful/frightening/longed-for content, they improve their ability to connect with their clients in their therapy sessions. Portrayals open up possibilities for supervisees to become more assertive, confident, and emotionally connected, and to engage in adaptive actions on behalf of themselves (Prenn, 2010).

In AEDP supervision, we use this tool to expand the possibilities of what a supervisee might say to a client. It is a way to start to formulate a response or a prompt; to put it into language; and to build new, expressive neural networks. The standard intervention is: "What would you want to say or do to let your client know how you feel about this if you could say or do anything at all without censoring?" It is a way to ask them to imagine—and thus experience—alternative ways of dealing with the client or ways to solve whatever dilemma the supervisee presents with. An even simpler intervention is: "What might you say?"

In the following vignette, notice the following skills in action: affirmation, modeling (supervisor models the intervention, describes possible interventions first), asking permission, and using imagination.

Supervisor: What might you say to Suzanna, your client? [**starting and modeling the use of portrayal**]

Supervisee: I don't know. I am having so much trouble with this client. She dodges my every intervention, she nods, sounds emotional. I think we are connecting and getting traction around something . . . and then she dismisses me with a wave of her hand, or a "yes, but!" And she moves right away from her emotions and me. I like her so much and understand how she came by her dismissive ways honestly, and yet I feel so shut out by her and so deskilled. I want to help her, and I just feel so pushed away by her!

Supervisor: I love what you just said. [**expressing delight in the supervisee**] I think you just said it! What could you say to her about all of this? [**affirming all supervisee is already doing**]

Supervisee: I don't know.

Supervisor: Well, you just so beautifully told me how you experience her. Could you imagine telling her? [**stretching the supervisee to just imagine**]

Supervisee: Telling her?

Supervisor: Yes, telling her . . . Tell her. If she was here right now, what would you say—what do you call her? Suzanna? Suzy? [**the standard way to start a portrayal with the immediacy of saying the client's name**]

Supervisee: I call her Suzy.

Supervisor: So you'd say, "Suzy, I like you so much and I feel shut out by you." What else would you say to her? [**Start the portrayal to actively help.**]

Supervisee: You dismiss me.

Supervisor: That's right. Keep going, tell her directly. [**affirm, offer encouragement**]

Supervisee: Suzy, you dismiss me. You nod and say, yes, and then, with a wave of your hand, you wipe me out. I feel invisible with you. I feel so small and like you don't see me.

Supervisor: That's right. How do you feel towards her?

Supervisee: I feel so whiplashed by you, like we are together and I am safe, and then off you go dismissing me, and I feel so abandoned in these moments with you [*looks a little surprised*]. Oh, I know this feeling—oh, I know where this comes from . . . huh. Okay.

Supervisor: What are you getting? What are you realizing? Is that okay to ask?

Supervisee: This is my stuff; my history. I know that this is coming from my childhood. I can tell you I know exactly where this comes from.

Supervisor: You can if you want, and for our purposes here, that isn't necessary.

Here, the supervisor encourages her supervisee to get deeper into her experience with her client to unpack the countertransference or the dynamics. Without her supervisor knowing the details from her past, the supervisee nevertheless sees the dynamics at play with her client, Suzy.

5. Integrative/Reflective Skills

Metaprocessing

This skill highlights what has felt good and has promoted growth in the session and in our work session-to-session. The explicit exploration together of the experience, skills, new learning, and answer to the supervisee's questions helps both supervisor and supervisee know and remember what has happened in their time together. Supervisors metaprocess throughout the supervision session and at the end of each session.

Platforming/Narrating

After an interpersonal moment in which a supervisee has broken eye contact, the supervisor inquires gently about the shift: "What just happened?" and the supervisee lets the supervisor know that what the supervisor had said was not helpful, and why. The supervisor takes a moment to *platform*, or sum up or recap, what happened so that once it's out there and shared, it can launch the next exploration:

> I noticed your breaking eye contact with me. It was a notice-and-seize moment. You let me know that what I was saying wasn't helpful to you and why and how that felt physically, and then we both noticed together we felt more relaxed and connected, and we metaprocessed how it was: "It was better . . . it was good," you said, and we both laughed about it. You told me what you needed; we both got color back in our cheeks! And now this is a bit of a teaching point: What did I do and how was it for you? And how are we now?

This platforming allows a right-brain experience to be interpreted by left-brain reflection and language, as described in Chapter 1.

Narrating/Thinking Out Loud/Voicing the Therapist

Conceição, Iwakabe, Edlin, et al. (2016) describe how supervisors share their thinking about videorecorded therapy sessions according to the experience level of the supervisee. With a beginning clinician, we might model this thinking aloud first and then ask the supervisee to join in and share his or her take. For a more seasoned clinician, we might ask that person to think aloud first, and then we might say, "Would it be okay if I added some of what I was noticing and thinking, and perhaps other ways of working?" Again, notice that asking permission is almost always a part of AEDP's supervisory offerings.

Eliciting Specific Feedback From the Supervisee

One of the most common challenges we all face is bringing up negative feedback, yet eliciting negative feedback from a supervisee is essential. Remember to ask, "How are we doing? How did we do today? What was helpful? What was not helpful?" AEDP does privilege the positive, but we also recognize the necessity of expanding a supervisee's ability to meta-process all aspects of a therapy session. In eliciting negative feedback, we use kindness; directness offered with tact; and "I" statements, rather than third-person deliveries of authoritative knowledge; and we always metaprocess the experience. As a part of this process, the supervisor should also check in about how the inquiry or intervention has landed. "You are having a reaction to my bringing it up?" Notice that we try to describe what is happening with curiosity, without judgment. It is likely that anxiety is driving the process, so we want to regulate that before we do anything else.

We elicit negative feedback in three different ways. First, we ask for specificity: "What specifically did not feel good for you about what I said?" "How did it affect you?" "You say you are not feeling heard. Can you give me an example?" We pursue concrete, practical examples, seeking to apply what was discussed in the supervisory hour.

Sometimes, in response to our requests for negative feedback, a supervisee or client will explain why we are not the supervisor or therapist for him or her, and this is useful information. We are not for everybody; we can try to be, and we can adapt and be creative, but sometimes there is too much of a mismatch. In response, the supervisor might say, "This is something I have heard before and know about myself." This is stating directly: "It is not your fault." This is a starting point and not an endpoint: We always try to metaprocess. These authentic moments feel good; they are real, not defended, and are open and engaged.

The second way we elicit negative feedback is by modeling the cycle of attunement, disruption, and repair (Safran & Muran, 2000; Tronick, 1998). We show that mistakes can be made and misattunement can occur. When we are not attuned (e.g., we intervene in a way that unintentionally shames or injures), we seek to repair. And because we metaprocess, we know it is happening and we can repair. This process models the cycle of disruption and repair, and also lets the supervisor know what is not helpful.

A third way we elicit negative feedback is through the use and understanding of nonverbal communication. A supervisee who shrugs her shoulders, twiddles her pen, or closes her computer may be having a reaction. This is a place to use our moment-to-moment tracking skill: "You are saying, 'Yes,' and you are also shrugging as you speak—what might your shoulders say if you let them?" or "I notice, and, correct me if I am wrong, some hesitancy as you say, 'Yes, I will try that.'"

The platforming intervention also may be particularly helpful here, as you might say, "Yes, this is helpful, and I see you get quiet and shrug your shoulder. [*Supervisor shrugs, too.*] I wonder what your body is saying." Or, "I notice that we spend a lot of time talking at the beginning of our sessions so that we don't always have enough time to watch the tape of your session with the client."

CONCLUSION

In this chapter—intended as a primer of essential skills—we highlighted the key elements of the AEDP supervisory stance and the skill set necessary for positive supervisory experiences. We expanded the theoretical idea of the true self and true other to describe the AEDP supervisor as a transformation other to the supervisee's transitional self. We translated AEDP theory into five kinds of user-friendly interventions and provided examples of actual interventions: (a) experiential skills, (b) privileging the positive skills, (c) relational skills, (d) affective/emotion-focused techniques, and (e) integrative/reflective skills. We encourage you to practice some of these skills in your supervisory sessions, if that feels right.

In the next chapter, you will see how the concepts and skills fit together as we examine, with annotated commentary, the transcript of a supervision session from beginning to end.

3

AEDP Supervision in Action: Microanalysis of an AEDP Supervision Session

Accelerated experiential dynamic psychotherapy (AEDP) is about change moments: how to bring them about and how to make the most of them when they occur. In supervision, we want to affirm and celebrate change for the better when it happens, and we want to clearly notice when it is not happening. Both—that is, when things go well and when things don't—present opportunities for us to teach and for supervisees to learn. The cocreation of relational safety and unwavering support for the supervisee is crucial. With aloneness undone, we can engage in deeper work and take more risks to allow learning to occur. It is what allows us to aim for rigor without shame.

The supervision session described in this chapter between Diana Fosha and supervisee Michael Glavin appears on the DVD *Accelerated Experiential Dynamic Psychotherapy (AEDP) Supervision* (Fosha, 2016), which is available for purchase from the American Psychological Association

http://dx.doi.org/10.1037/0000016-004
Supervision Essentials for Accelerated Experiential Dynamic Psychotherapy, by N. C. N. Prenn and D. Fosha

(https://www.apa.org/pubs/videos/4310958.aspx). In this session, we discover that with trust established, relaxation and deepening follow. We see this in the client, supervisee, and supervisor. Here, we witness a deepening of the troubling material that needs to be worked through along with the distressing affects that go with it. We also witness a deepening of confidence, well-being, calm, and clarity, and the positive affects that go with those experiences.

OPENING MOMENTS OF THE SUPERVISION SESSION

Diana: Hi, Michael.

Michael: Hi, Diana.

Diana: Nice to see you.

Michael: It's good to see you again.

Diana: Looking forward to doing this piece of work together.

Michael: Me, too.

These may seem like mere social niceties, but starting with a warm welcome is important. Neither severe nor neutral, the supervisor actively expresses pleasure at being with her supervisee. Gershen Kaufman (1996), who wrote one of the best books on shame and how to transform it, spoke of the importance of the child seeing the delight on the parent's face and feeling the parent's own desire to be with the child. When the attachment figure (here, the supervisor) initiates the interaction, it is an anti-shame inoculation: The recipient feels "I am wanted," "I count." In this seemingly prosaic exchange, we have an example of the attachment-based stance from the get-go: The supervisor leads, and her message is, "I want to do this work with you, and I am glad you exist."

Diana: Yeah. So, maybe we can begin by hearing something about [your client]. [**Supervisor takes the lead in structuring and organizing the interaction.**] [*Michael*: "Sure."] And then we'll take it from there.

Michael: That sounds good. This is Amy. This is only the third session I'm having with her. This is really early work. She came in because her husband recently left her and wants a divorce. And so she's feeling confused and frustrated and sad; also, it's not really clear why he wants a divorce, and so that's throwing her.

Diana: I see, so it's not clear to *her*. [**striving for specificity**]

Michael: Yeah, there's not any one reason. She's a bit concerned about how he's doing. He's lost a lot of weight, he's not sleeping; his friends—mutual friends—are telling her that they're worried about him. She doesn't want the divorce, but he's really adamant about getting a divorce, and so she's sort of caught and asking me, "What do I do?"

Diana: Great. Not great, not great at all, but thank you for making it clear.

Supervision also is about the supervisor's getting to know the client and getting a feel for the client and his or her issues and dynamics so the supervisor is able to properly guide the supervisee.

Diana: So . . . she's dealing with two things, really: One is the pain of the divorce but also being worried about him, confused. [*Michael: "Right. Right."*] I guess it's early, it's just the third session, but anything of the context [for this session] that we should sort of put in that will help us? [**beginning of *we* language**]

Michael: Yeah, the previous session, she was talking about her frustration. She's having a hard time coping. She's functional, but she's missing work. She's getting overwhelmed with emotion a lot, so she's sort of collapsing a lot. In the previous session, I thought maybe if she got in touch with her anger that could help her sort of steady herself and get more functional. She sort of mentioned it, but then we couldn't get to it, but we got to sort of grieving, and so we did some grieving work in the last session, which was great.

The supervisor's question allows the supervisee to bring in what's on his mind. The supervisee has concerns about his client's functionality, and, in his mind, there is some unfinished business from the prior session. He is implicitly expressing his concern for his client and also is wondering if he did right by her. He wouldn't want to contribute to her compromised functionality by not helping her process some intense and dysregulated feelings. His statement suggests he has something of an agenda: to get back to feelings not fully dealt with. It's an AEDP agenda because AEDP is emotion focused and about helping and accompanying clients to tolerate, regulate, and process their overwhelming emotions.

Diana: Okay. And what is she grieving?

Michael: Uh, the loss of the relationship. And, so, in this session—as I set up this clip—we'll get to the questions in a second—she mentions frustration again. We do a little bit of work on frustration, where she's able to drop into the core affect and then she sort of pops out of it again and says, "I have to accept what's happening and move on." I sort of want to bring her back. I want to sort of validate her feelings, try to help deal with the shame, and to help her drop down, and then try to get back to the frustration, so that's what I'm gonna be doing in this clip.

Diana: Okay. Thank you.

In saying, "Thank you," the supervisor affirms the supervisee for being focused and clear, and for volunteering his questions. In AEDP supervision, we want the supervision session structured through the lens of a specific question of concern to the supervisee, which organizes our focus from the multiplicity of pathways that could be taken.

Michael: She cycles pretty quickly, going from . . . frustration . . . to "I shouldn't be feeling this way," with inhibitory affects of shame or guilt, and then she'll go back to sadness, and the sadness will then give way to something else. One question is: How much should I be slowing her down to deepen her work, and how much should I just continue to track her and follow her along as she goes, cycles? [**The supervisee organizes his questions in terms of the triangle of experience.**]

The supervisee is doing really well: He has come in with a specific question and declares his understanding in the terms of the triangle of experience. The supervisor (Fosha) notices that he is focused on the importance of frustration. Within the differential phenomenology of the transformational process, frustration is not a core affect that we want to deepen; rather, we want to transform it into a core affect. At this point, it is unclear whether the supervisee is distinguishing between frustration as a mixed state (State 1) and anger as a core emotion (State 2). The supervisor holds this in mind as the process unfolds. She notes the importance of frustration to the supervisee and wants to reserve judgment until seeing the phenomenology on the video clip. The supervisee has a question; now, the supervisor does, as well.

Michael: And then . . . in the later part of the tape, I start to become an advocate for her [*Diana: "Mmm."*] because she's doubting herself and going through this. So I pick up some of what she said, and I reflect that back to her in a really kind of strong way. [*Diana: "Right."*] And so my question: Is that okay? Am I doing it too much?

Diana: Got it.

Michael: I keep checking in with her to see how it is for her, but—

Diana: How the validation/affirmation is going, right?

Michael: Yeah. Yeah. And so I want to see what your sense is about that, and we can talk about that.

Advocacy on behalf of the client in the face of the client's own self-judgment is an important part of AEDP work (Lamagna, 2016). However, for it to be effective, it has to be attuned. The supervisee's question is an excellent one: Is his advocacy to Amy on behalf of Amy clinically indicated? Is it attuned? Is it excessive? Is he missing anything important when he is busy affirming her? The process helps us answer his question.

Diana: That sounds good. We'll go about this like the usual AEDP supervision. You selected these clips. We'll look at them, and either you or I can choose to stop the tape if there's something we want to discuss or something you have a question about or I have a question about. [**being explicit about how they will proceed—and emphasizing the collaborative nature of the supervision, as well as the moment-to-moment nature of the process—either the supervisor or the supervisee can stop the tape if they see something that they want to address**]

Michael: Great. Sounds good. [*Diana: "Cool."*] What we're gonna see is the last 11 minutes of the session.

THERAPY VIGNETTE 1

Client: That frustration is gonna be the hardest for me to let go of. [*cries*]

Therapist: Right.

Client: [*pauses, takes deep breath, smiles*]

Therapist: It's okay to feel feelings.

Client: [*nods*] Mmm.

Therapist: Right now.

Client: Yeah. [*nods*]

Therapist: You're in a very frustrating situation, and you can't do anything, right now.

Client: Yeah. [*nods, smiles*]

[*Diana talks while therapy tape is rolling: "Nice big smile there."*]

Therapist: It's not your fault. You blame yourself, and then you can't fix it, and it's really frustrating.

Client: Yeah. [*nods*]

Therapist: [*nods*] Yeah, so what's happening?

Client: I'm hoping that it's just something that goes away with time. [*chuckles*]

SUPERVISION, POST THERAPY VIGNETTE 1

Michael: So, my read is she's gone up the triangle to the inhibitory affect. [**speaking the language of the triangle of experience**]

Diana: Inhibitory affect, meaning . . . ?

Michael: I think she feels bad about feeling frustrated in the situation, and I think there's a little bit of shame in there.

Diana: I see, so that—okay. Yeah, go ahead.

Michael: I'm trying to validate her: "Of course you feel frustrated; this is a frustrating situation—all of a sudden someone's asking you for a divorce and you don't know why." I'm trying to help deal with that inhibitory affect so that she can then drop down, hopefully into the core affect of frustration or anger.

Diana: Yeah. Right. A couple of things. One is I think it's inhibitory affect but it's a little bit of "common wisdom." Not so much the spiritual bypass, but "we have to move to acceptance." [**the supervisor has a somewhat different take from the supervisee on what the client is doing—not a contradictory one, but different**] [*Michael: "Right, right, right."*] But, as you tune into her having trouble accepting the situation, you really affirm her. And don't just affirm, you actually talk a fair amount, so it's a little bit of psycho-ed. [*Michael: "Mmm."*] [**translating supervisee's interventions into the language of AEDP**]

In the first of many such supervision interventions, the supervisor narrates to the supervisee what he is doing from her perspective, that is, in the language of AEDP. That is what Conceição and colleagues (Conceição, Rodrigues, Silva, et al., 2016; Rodrigues, Conceição, Iwakabe, & Gleiser, 2015) called *voicing the therapist*. As she does this here, she sees that she has his endorsement. The supervisor is talking as though he already knows this, which he almost does. In the 1670 play *Le Bourgeois Gentilhomme* (*The Bourgeois Gentleman*, Timothy Mooney adaptation) by Molière, a character says, "What do you know? These forty years, I have been speaking prose without knowing it." In that spirit, a central AEDP intervention in both therapy and supervision is to take something that seems scary for the client or daunting for the supervisee and show them how they are already doing it.

Diana: Also, for somebody who has difficulty regulating her feelings, you're providing—starting to provide—a strong container. [**validation and education**] [*Michael: "Right."*] "I'm here. I'm saying this, there's this and that." And then, because we still don't know what she will—how she will—react, you ask her, you check in with her: "What is it like to hear," right? [*Michael: "Right."*] [**voicing the therapist; that is, narrating the supervisee's actions from the supervisor's perspective**]

Diana: It's this first pass, and she says it's sort of—

Michael: And she misses everything I said. [*Both Michael and Diana laugh.*]

Diana: Right, it's: "Nice, but meh!"

Michael: Yeah, she says, "I'm hoping that's something that can go away with time." [*Diana: "Right."*] She's still in that "let's just move along, let's not get frustrated, let's not deal with this affect."

Diana: Right [*nods*]. Right.

The therapist makes an intervention that both he and the supervisor like. Nevertheless, the client's response tells us that she's not touched by it. An intervention is useful only if it is received. The therapist processes that information in real time and uses it to inform his next intervention. So, Michael decides to up the relational ante.

Michael: Then I start thinking: Okay, she missed what I said, so I start using *we* language and then sort of ask permission. [**lovely application of AEDP principle of using a relational intervention to see if a defense can be bypassed**] "Can we drop down, deal with some of this frustration?" That's what we'll see next. [**indicates that he is categorizing frustration as a core affect, which is an issue the supervisor will need to address**]

Diana: A couple of comments. Again, we're tracking two things: We're tracking affect and emotion, and how she's dealing with frustration—and by the way, the word *frustration* already connotes that she's at the top of the triangle.

Michael: [*nods*] Right.

Diana: Frustration is some mixture of something; it's very different than anger.

Michael: Right. Right. [**The supervisor, for now, gets the affective thumbs up from the supervisee.**]

Diana: We're tracking the affect in one track, and we're also tracking the relational component. Right? [*Michael: "Mmm. Right."*] And you're doing both really very beautifully. [**affirmation, focus on what supervisee is doing well**]

Michael: [*smiles*] Thank you. [**positive somatic–affective marker; the smile signals receptivity, that is, he is taking in what the supervisor is saying to him**]

Diana: You're smiling. [**It is important to metaprocess "a moment of in-supervision session experience," a moment marked by positive affect.**]

Michael: [*smiles*] It just feels good to have your validation and recognition.

Diana: [*smiles*] Yeah. Yeah. Alright.

The positive affect signals that the process is on track; it also fuels motivation and deepens capacity to take risks. Relationships are built on such moments, and the motivation to explore, risk, and be open is forged from such moments.

THERAPY VIGNETTE 2

Therapist: We can work on it together. [*They nod to each other.*] Would you be open to doing that?

Client: [*nods*] Yeah. Yeah. Yeah.

Therapist: Are you still feeling that frustration?

Client: Yeah. Right now I feel what I need to be able to release that frustration is to better understand his point of view, or what he's thinking, and then that is even more frustrating because I don't think I'm ever gonna get it.

Therapist: Right.

Client: Which then just makes it more frustrating. [*smiling, uses both hands to grip the air in front of her*]

Therapist: [*mimics gesture*] What do your hands wanna do?

Client: [*shakes head, smiles*]

Therapist: Do you want a pillow to—[*makes gripping gesture*]

Client: [*laughs*] No. This is my gesture. [*repeats gesture, laughs*]

Diana talks while therapy tape is rolling: "She gets a little self-conscious."

Therapist: Right. But that's really expressive. [*repeats gesture, grits teeth*]

Client: Yeah.

Therapist: I'm imagining you grabbing him and shaking him or something. What are you thinking?

Diana talks while therapy tape is rolling: "Let's stop for a second."

SUPERVISION, POSTTHERAPY VIGNETTE 2

Diana: Great, she articulates something clearly. She says she wants to understand, [*Michael: "Mmm."*] and then she starts to talk about the frustration, and she makes this gesture. [*Michael: "Right."*] I was very curious to see what would happen, because, to me, she's still so much in State 1 that I wanted to see: *Can* she go with you? [*Michael: "Mmm. Right."*] Or not? And we get an answer.

This is an important teaching moment. The therapist's work suggests that he thinks his client is at the edge of State 2, and he is trying some experiential interventions for processing core emotion. The supervisor stops the tape to introduce the idea that, as a rule, one can't do experiential anger work with a client who still is in State 1. That is something that's been on the supervisor's mind since the supervisee introduced his concerns with frustration. Now, an opportunity has arisen, and thus the time has arrived to make it explicit. The supervisor's challenge here is how to teach and stay rigorous without shaming the supervisee. The phenomenology of the client's response often provides the answer to the question and needs to be registered. Therapists have to learn how to read those cues and adjust their therapeutic strategies. Instead of telling the therapist that he is mistaken, together we track and process his client's response to his interventions, and allow the process to provide us with the answers.

Michael: Right.

Diana: What do you think? [**fostering supervisee's initiative and getting the supervisee to make the implicit explicit**]

Note that this is an instance of parallel process: Just as the therapist needs to read his client to have a sense of how she is receiving him—or not—the supervisor needs to have a sense of how the supervisee is responding to what she is teaching him—or not.

Michael: In this moment it was "no."

Diana: Right.

Michael: She just disowned it, and said she's just a hand-talker—she wasn't doing this [*shows an angry grip*]; she was just doing *that*. [*shows a more casual form of the gesture*]

Diana: Right.

This exchange demonstrates the importance of tracking the client's response to the intervention moment-to-moment and using the new data to inform or shape the next intervention. Teaching this skill in supervision deepens the therapist's understanding of client dynamics.

Michael: And then I say what my experience imagining was, with her, and then she has nervous laughter about that.

Diana: Right. I think that she also got embarrassed. I think sometimes people get embarrassed when we reflect them, or mirror them.

A rule of improvisation is to never say, "No, but . . ." and instead, say, "Yes, and . . ." Here, the supervisor's use of "also" is equivalent to the "yes, and . . ." The client's embarrassment was not the effect the therapist was going for in raising the client's awareness of her body language. Nevertheless it is what happened; it must be named and we must make use of it.

Michael: Right. Right.

Diana: What I liked about what you did is that you said you did this [*grips the air tensely*], and she started to giggle, and you went right into a sort of stronger sense of what this gesture was about, you really put yourself in it. [**validation of the therapist's next intervention**]

Michael: Right.

Diana: I think even though it's not an overt shame intervention, at least, subliminally, I think you picked up on her shame, and just sort of said, "No, no, no, it's not that you talk funny, it's—" [**voices the therapist**]

The supervisor is affirming the therapist's next move and suggesting that it can be seen as an intuitive attempt to repair a minidisruption of the embarrassment or shame the client felt, even if that was not the conscious intention behind the intervention.

Michael: Right, right, right.

Diana: There's something strong here. But for the moment.

Michael: I feel like I'm trying to give her permission to feel some of that anger, if it is there.

Notice how the supervisee's awareness and language are changing: He is now speaking of anger and not frustration; and he is saying, "If it is there," which suggests that he is beginning to take in that maybe his client is not primarily angry and that something else may be going on.

THERAPY VIGNETTE 3

Client: [*smiles*] Today, I wanna say [*uses shaking gesture*], "You have to make sense! This does not make sense!"

Therapist: Yeah. Yeah. This does not make sense.

Client: Yeah.

Therapist: And can you imagine shaking him and saying, "This does not make sense! You have to make sense!"?

Client: Yes. Yes.

Therapist: And how does that feel to imagine shaking him and yelling at him?

Client: [*sighs, chuckles*] Well, it's good, [**positive somatic–affective marker**] but then I—but there's a "but."

The issue here is a common one: The therapist has an idea of what the client is, or should be, feeling, which, in this case is reasonable enough anger at the husband, who is wanting to divorce her out of the blue. However, the client seems to be on a different track. She needs her world to make sense, and what is happening doesn't really make sense to her. How this will be negotiated in the therapy, and also in the supervision, is a key question.

Michael: I felt she was able to drop a little bit down to the core affect. I felt that she really touched into State 2. And then I asked her how that felt, and then she takes that sigh [*sighs*]. And then she goes to "but."

SUPERVISION, POSTTHERAPY VIGNETTE 3

Diana: Right. And she calls it. She calls herself on it.

Michael: I feel I'm at this decision point: Where do I go?

This is a wonderful opportunity: The therapist bravely and honestly speaks of his sense of being lost at this moment, the "where do I go?" moment. Although he is still holding on to the primacy of working with the client's frustration, this crossroad—"where do I go?"—presents a great opportunity for teaching and learning.

Diana: Let's hold on to the decision point for a moment, just to talk about this a little bit. This is one of those fascinating things that happen. Even though your goal is to help her feel more of the core anger [*Michael: "Right."*] and you're working with a portrayal—and the hands, and getting the body, the visceral sense [*Michael: "Right."*]—it doesn't quite go to the frustration. You don't have the sense that she really wants to shake him. [*Michael: "Mmm."*] But the sense that I got is that there was an experience of recognition. Now she—as a result of the whole thing being more visceral and more somatic, and her being less in her head—she gets a piece of what's important to her. She gets that she needs to understand, that the world needs to make sense to her.

Through the moment-to-moment tracking and processing, a new understanding is emerging. Instead of telling the therapist what he should have done and how he ought to be perceiving what is happening, which can be quite shaming, the supervisor, instead, moves to say, "This is how I see this." She speaks of her evolving sense of what's important for the client. It is the supervisor's sense that the client is not struggling with anger turned inward, or anger to which she doesn't feel entitled, or anger that she fears. Rather, the supervisor's sense is that the client is struggling with needing to make sense of things and that her frustration is secondary to the fact that nothing of what's happening makes any sense to her. The supervisor is introducing this alternative understanding of the process and is doing it in the form of an "I" statement: "This is how I see it."

Diana: You had one intention, and it didn't quite go there, but it yielded something else.

Michael: Right.

We learn from what goes wrong, so to speak, as well as from what goes right. In the process of the client's rejecting one focus (frustration and the work pointing toward the need for the direct experience and expression of anger), another focus—one of great importance to the client—comes to the fore (i.e., the need for things to make sense). The supervisor wants to emphasize to the supervisee that his client's rejection of his focus is not a rejection of him; rather, it is an opportunity to fine-tune and understand better what's really the right focus for her so that he can better help her.

Diana: What's your sense at this point of what the choice is, given that we've done this little trajectory?

Michael: You know, there's the frustration, which I think is—I'm ruling that out as an option 'cause I think that moment has passed.

Diana: Right. I'm with you on that.

Phew. The therapist is letting go of the frustration, an agenda he had since the previous session. Through the process they have undergone, he is articulating that he is letting go of his previous agenda of his own volition. The supervisor supports his statement.

Michael: I think if I had to do it again, I would go with the sigh 'cause there was some relief that something happened. I would wanna investigate that a little bit, or see if I could investigate that.

Wonderful. Our supervisory process is yielding creativity, flexibility, and self-supervision. The supervisee now sees an alternate focus: the sigh, that is, the somatic–affective marker of relief that indicates that something therapeutic occurred for the client.

Diana: A little change moment.

Michael: Right, a second state transformation. What is *in* that relief?

Diana: Right.

Michael: I'm also aware that I don't know what that *but* is—where that is going. This is only the third session.

The supervisee is on a roll. He and the supervisor have cocreated safety in the supervisory relationship. He knows that even if he's not perfect, he will not be shamed here. So now his exploratory drive is coming to the fore: His curiosity and his deep wish to do well by his client are in the driver's seat.

Michael: I want to wind up asking, "Where's she going now?" I want to keep moving with her, keep tracking her.

Diana: I want to validate what you did in this session. Even though there's the sigh and there's the *yes*, there's a sense that there's something else in the picture, so maybe going for the *but* will let you fold in that she's sort of divided.

Michael: Right.

Diana: She's trying to be with you. [**The supervisor puts in a good word for the client's striving for transformance.**] I like that.

Michael: Okay. Well, we'll see what happens. [*chuckles*] [**wonderful attitude of openness and curiosity**]

Diana: Let's see what happens.

THERAPY VIGNETTE 4

Therapist: What else is there?

Client: I know that I'm not gonna get what I want from that. It's not gonna make sense.

Therapist: Right. He's not gonna make sense.

Client: No. And even if he thinks it's making sense, it's not gonna make sense to me.

Therapist: Right. [*They nod.*]

SUPERVISION, POSTTHERAPY VIGNETTE 4

Michael: [*pauses video*] She says, "It's not gonna make sense." I say, "He's not gonna make sense." And then, I want to locate that in space—that there's a difference there, that they're gonna have two different versions of what's going on.

Diana: Right. And we're getting the "making sense" again as this theme of what she needs.

Michael: Right. Right.

Diana: If she can't have the marriage, at least she can have some coherence. [**elaboration of emerging theme**]

Michael: Right. Right. And I see her now starting to collapse again. It's not making sense, and then tears come up, and she seems to be getting dysregulated, right? [*Diana: "Right."*] I don't know what to do. [*laughs*]

The supervisee now has trust enough and feels comfortable enough to be direct about his being at a loss for what to do in session. This is a huge moment in the supervision! We all have felt at a loss, but how often do we feel safe enough and comfortable enough to say it directly? [**This is a change moment in the supervision.**] The supervisor will reflect that back and try to make explicit what she sees is happening.

Diana: Right.

Michael: If you have a different—yeah, I'd be interested to hear a different way to work here in this moment where she goes to that "but it's not gonna make sense," and then she starts to get dysregulated.

The supervisee follows his self-disclosure of being at a loss by a direct request for alternatives. Alternatives offered by the supervisor now will be in response to his request and not taken as criticisms.

Diana: I wanted to just appreciate, you know, your honesty, and your being direct about, "I don't know what to do." [**The supervisor makes the implicit explicit: I name *and* appreciate this wonderful new development. I mark it with my recognition.**]

Michael: Yeah.

Diana: We all feel that. [**normalize, universalize, use *we* language**] You know, there's so much going on, the client's dysregulating—there are several things and that internal sense, your being able to share that with me. I really appreciate that. [*Michael smiles, nods.*] [**affirmation of relational risk-taking**] I think it took courage. You know, particularly [because] we're on tape, it ups the ante, so it took even more courage.

Validate. Appreciate. Normalize. Affirm. And then metaprocess. Bring in the unique feature of the moment, which is that we are doing this session in front of cameras for worldwide distribution. To call it intimidating is an understatement, all of which makes the supervisee's courage all the more remarkable.

Michael: [*smiles wider, chuckles*] I appreciate you saying that. [**positive somatic–affective markers**]

Diana: Can you stay with that just for a second? What it's like to have me say, "We all struggle with that." [**We are now metaprocessing a huge positive change moment in the here-and-now of the supervision.**] It's an intellectual question, but secondly, it's a brave thing to do. [*nods*]

Michael: It feels like I'm recognized and being seen, and validated. The sharing of it feels good. I'm glad I did.

Diana: Stay with "it's feeling good" for one more moment. It's a little paradoxical—something that's hard but feels good.

Michael: Right. It feels relaxing in here [*places hand over chest*] and a calming openness. [*They both nod.*] Excitement. [**positive somatic–affective markers in the supervisee**]

Diana: Yeah. When you said that, I actually felt myself [*takes deep breath*] take a breath and drop down. [**positive somatic–affective markers in the supervisor**]

Diana: All right, shall we go back to Amy?

This is an instance of the broaden-and-build theory of positive emotion (Fredrickson, 2001, 2009) in action in moment-to-moment AEDP supervision. As often happens in metaprocessing, we have positive affects in the person who's having the transformational experience—here, the supervisee; dyadic resonance and affective contagion when the other member of the dyad—here, the supervisor—also experiences positive affects; and through the resonance, amplification leads to upward, positive spirals of positive affect and energy that fuel the process, which, aptly enough, continues here with further exploration. We have established a new, higher baseline of connection, honesty, and learning, which leads to mutual positive affect, more energy, and new understanding. The dyadic system has been upgraded; now, more can be accomplished in the supervision.

Michael: Yeah, I see her dysregulating, and I'm not sure what to do, so I just reflect back what I'm seeing with her and just see what she makes of it.

Diana: Okay. Always a good strategy. [**validation of his using close tracking to reorient**] We let ourselves know what's going on as we're letting the client know what's going on. [**support, *we* language, universalizing the difficult experience**]

THERAPY VIGNETTE 5

Therapist: Does that resonate with you?

Client: [*nods*] A little. [*smiles*] 'Cause I think I know that I'm not gonna get what I need from him; and then it comes back to me, being frustrated, that I think that I need that to be able to [*some tears well up*].

Therapist: So you get frustrated with yourself. [*Client chuckles, nods.*] You think that you need him to make sense.

Client: Yeah. Yeah. Yeah, why do I [*tears well up*], why do I feel I need to understand? Well, of course I want to be able to understand why my marriage is dissolving.

Therapist: Yeah. Yeah, yeah.

Client: But why do I need to understand to be okay?

SUPERVISION, POSTTHERAPY VIGNETTE 5

Michael: This is gonna set up the next part where she's questioning herself, and this is where, I think she gets dysregulated—not just here, but in everyday life, just starts to get overwhelmed, and the feelings come up and then she feels bad about having the feelings and wants to understand, and feels bad that she wants to understand. [*Diana, nods: "Right."*] I pick up part of that, and I just wanna sort of advocate for her—"of course you want to know, of course you want to make sense of this"—because I sort of want to help contain her and keep her from spinning out.

Diana: I think you're doing a great job, you know, using the relational interventions here, and this goes back to your first question about slowing her down. I might have wanted to do that—to try it and see whether she is able to be sufficiently present to take in what you're asking her, because she's doing the work, but with a lot of anxiety.

Michael: Right. Right.

Diana: I would be curious to say, "Okay, I really hear you. But can we just take a breath and just slow it down?" [*speaks in a slowed-down voice*] Right? Just in this way, so that your voice then carries that message to her. [**suggestions for alternative interventions in the form of an "I" statement, and experiential modeling; that is, the supervisor actually does what she is urging him to do and slows down her speech**] [*Michael nods: "Yeah. Yeah."*] I would have tried that.

Michael: Yeah, that's helpful. [*nods*]

Diana: You're taking the relational route and the meaning route, the coherence route, because she's also articulating something about that.

Again, the one, two, "yes, and . . ." intervention: first an affirmation, and a sincere one, because he is indeed doing an excellent job, and then the new thing—the alternate pathway expressed in "I" language, expressed as a possibility and not as the missed intervention. Instead of saying, "You should have slowed her down here" or "you might have wanted to slow her down here," what the supervisor says is, "I might have wanted to help her slow her down here." And then another affirmation. This as an alternative path sandwich on affirmation bread.

Michael: Right. Right.

Diana: Yeah. Great.

Michael: Great.

Diana: All right.

This back-and-forth of "great" communicates that the supervisor and supervisee are on the same page—they are in tune, the supervisory process is moving, both of them feel together, and both feel good about it. The supervisee takes the supervisor's suggestion, internalizes it, and practices it in his own words. The supervisor is gaining confidence in herself as a supervisor in this moment, with her supervisee in the process in which they are engaged. The supervisor's own anxiety or apprehension with which she entered the supervision session is dissipating. And both supervisor and supervisee are beginning to have fun, which is paradoxical, given the client's distress and the therapist struggles and worries. That's one of the quintessential aspects of metaprocessing: even difficult things, when shared and met with responsiveness, feel good. This is the true self–true other relating in action.

Let's review what four accomplishments have been achieved thus far: (a) The supervisee and supervisor have cocreated safety and have been engaged in undoing the aloneness of the therapist/supervisee. (b) With safety achieved and mutual trust growing, there is more openness to risk-taking and learning. With each round, with more resonance and positive energy, the system of both participants—and that of the supervisory dyad—is getting upgraded so that there is greater capacity to do the work. (c) The supervisee is able to hear new things, alternative ways of thinking and intervening, and can explore them—even embrace them—without feeling shame or shamed for not having come up with them on his own. (d) The process has precision and specificity. Both supervisor and supervisee are getting to know this client and what she needs, and they are learning from and making use of what is going well and what is not working.

Michael: The next part—and this is sort of a long part—it's 5 minutes or so; stop it whenever you want.

Diana: Okay, we might stop. Right. Thank you.

Michael: My question is about advocacy. As I was [responding to her], I was thinking, "Is this too much?" or "Is this too far?" I say things like, "Everybody wants that, of course you want that, everybody—" [**The supervisee restates a question he introduced at the beginning, but which directly applies to the next vignette they are about to watch.**]

Michael: I say it pretty strongly. I ask her, "How is it to hear that?" I'm checking in with her, but I just wanna see what your sense is. Do I do it too much, or are there [other] ways that would be effective? [**He is heralding his intervention and is explicitly asking for the supervisor's input, her "sense" of what and how he is doing.**]

Diana: Right, and we'll track it together. I'll stop it, but you feel free to stop it also if you see something that you didn't see before. [**This is yet another opportunity for the supervisor to emphasize the collaborative nature of the supervisory enterprise in AEDP.**] [*Michael: "Okay."*] Because for us to answer that question is not an abstract "it is too much" or "you never do it when . . ." Right? [*Michael: "Right. Right."*] Let's track how it's landing. [**The only answer to the question "Is this the right intervention?" is in the client's response.**]

THERAPY VIGNETTE 6

Client: [*cries and then pauses*]

Therapist: Of course you want to understand. [*Client nods.*] Does that make sense?

Client: [*nods*]

Therapist: I mean, everybody wants to understand their marriage—to know what happened or why it happened.

Client: Yeah. [*nods*]

Therapist: So, of course you want to know that. [**validation**]

Client: That's actually calming. [**change moment in the therapy**]

[*Diana talks while therapy tape is rolling: "Said from the heart, that's nice. Let's stop for a second."*]

SUPERVISION POSTTHERAPY VIGNETTE 6

Diana: So that's really—clearly that gets taken in.

Diana: This is really the first moment that we've watched together. [*takes deep breath, sighs*]

Michael: Yeah.

Diana: I mean, we had *our* moment of calming, but now she does. I think it's 'cause it's impassioned and it's personal. [**meaning that what you, Michael, say, is said with passion, authenticity, deep feeling**]

Michael: Mmm.

Diana: You say, "everybody"; in other words, *all* of us would want to know.

Michael: Right.

Diana: And she says, "That's actually calming."

Michael: Yeah. And, looking again, I think that helps with the shame. It's not just you that wants to know that, but "everybody, of course."

Diana: Exactly. There's nothing wrong with you for wanting this; it's a universal human experience. We're all in it together. And, I think it's that you're speaking in an impassioned way.

Michael: Mmm. Yeah.

Diana: In a way, she finally lands and makes contact with you.

Michael: Right. Right.

Diana: This is the first moment that it's contact, and you're able to sort of—for a moment, she calms down.

Michael: [*nods*]

Diana: Yeah. So, very nice. Very nice. I know you said 5 minutes, that we have more to watch, but this is an important moment. [**impassioned affirmation and praise for the supervisee**]

Michael: Yeah. Right. That feels good. [*smiles*] [**positive somatic–affective markers in the supervisee**]

The supervisor notes the positive moment, yet it is important to the supervisee to show the 5 minutes, so the supervisor is tabling the good feeling, trusting that she and the supervisee will have more opportunities for processing and metaprocessing the positive affects arising out of the supervisory process.

THERAPY VIGNETTE 7

Client: 'Cause I deserve it [to know why her husband wants to leave] . . . like . . . [**change moment in the therapy**]

Michael: Yeah, you do.

[*Diana talks while therapy tape is rolling: "Wow!"*]

Client: That was the deal. [*chuckles*]

Therapist: You really deserved that, right.

Client: Yeah.

Therapist: You deserve to know what happened and why, and what's going on.

[*Diana talks while therapy tape is rolling. "Right."*]

Therapist: And it's frustrating that you don't.

Client: And I think, too, when you say that, I think I'm not doing a good enough job of accepting, or listening, and accepting his reasoning, or what he thinks—well, what he thinks his reasoning is, what he believes to have happened.

[*Diana talks while therapy tape is rolling: "Can we stop for a second?"*]

Michael: Yeah.

SUPERVISION POSTTHERAPY VIGNETTE 7

Diana: As we often see in AEDP, the person gets calm, deepens, and then the next round . . . [**moment-to-moment phenomenological tracking of state shift, and its therapeutic aftermath**]

Michael: [*nods*] Right. Right.

Diana: And what struck me is right after the calm she said something like, "I deserve that." [**highlighting a crucial, not to be missed, moment**]

Michael: Right.

Diana: So that's an implicit antishame—I mean, it's very antishame, but implicit to whatever she was feeling before, when she actually volunteers, "I deserve that." That's a *big* statement.

Michael: [*tilts head*] [**a marker of openness, receptivity, wonder**] Right. Right.

It is essential to mark, that is, notice and seize, moments of change for the better and not let them go by unnoticed. These moments are crucial to AEDP's mechanisms of therapeutic action. The phenomenological moment-to-moment tracking in conditions of dyadic safety in the supervision is bearing fruit: The supervisory dyad has a moment of revelation, and the supervisee has a genuine moment of deep understanding about his client's dynamics; the head tilt marks his new learning.

Diana: Yeah.

Michael: Yeah. [*smiles*] [**positive somatic–affective markers in the supervisee**]

Diana: I keep seeing that nice smile. [*They laugh.*] Yeah, tell me?

Having not seized the previous positive affect in the here-and-now of the supervision, the supervisor and supervisee are going here for both the supervisee's positive affect at being recognized, at seeing the positive moment of change in the therapy, and at deepening his understanding of his client—with the insight that just emerged about the undoing of the client's shame.

Michael: That's a big recognition, which didn't click. My intuition, and also in preparing this tape and looking at it, was, "I *think* she's feeling shame," with the [assumption that we] *should* move on that. [*Diana: "Right."*] But what you're saying, that's a validation that she was feeling shame; "I deserve it" is an antishame thing. Okay, that helps me understand what she was feeling before in that swirl of everything else. [**coherent narrative of his understanding of his client**]

Diana: Exactly. Yeah. And the big smile. [*smiles*] [**positive somatic–affective markers in the supervisor**]

Michael: That's very helpful.

Diana: Yeah?

Michael: It's validating, but it's also—I can use this—in this relationship with her and my work with her.

Diana: Great. You can take it back with you. [*Michael: "Yeah, yeah, yeah."*]

The dual purpose of AEDP supervision is accomplished: Not only does the supervisee feel validated but he also learned something deep about his client that he didn't know before and that will help him in the therapy with her going forward. It is exciting to add that, in an email to Diana while he was reviewing a transcript of this supervisory session for this book, Michael said that he realized that in this moment, he experienced his "intellectual aloneness" as being undone. This realization expands AEDP supervision theory in that it adds intellectual aloneness to emotional aloneness. And its antidote, which we meet here, is the excitement when we feel accompanied intellectually and emotionally.

Diana: Sometimes it is that way with shame—with other affects, too, but I think particularly shame, since it's so hidden, that you sort of know about it when it's over. [**a teaching moment about shame**]

Michael: Right. Right.

Diana: All right, but we're now on to the next chapter and she's blaming herself. She ought to be doing something different than what she's doing.

Michael: Right.

THERAPY VIGNETTE 8

Client: ... in a place where I'm responding to it with my own memory and thought of what happened.

Therapist: Right.

[*Diana talks while therapy tape is rolling: "Mmm."*]

Therapist: And, of course you are.

Client: [*nods*] Yeah.

Therapist: Right?

Client: Like, yeah. And then I'm frustrated that I feel I have to be the one that says, "Okay, I believe you, sure."

Therapist: Yeah. But you don't.

Client: But I don't. [*smiles, nods*]

Therapist: And that's okay to not believe him.

Client: Yeah. [*nods, crying*] [**change moment in the therapy**]

Therapist: Right, that's okay. Right? [*Client nods.*] It's okay. How's that to hear?

[*Diana talks while therapy tape is rolling: "That did raise her affect."*]

Client: I don't know if I believe you. [*laughs*]

Therapist: [*nods*]

Client: But it has to be. Yeah.

Therapist: You have your own experience of what happened. Right? [*Client nods.*] You have your own, right. He's saying something that really contradicts your own lived experience. [*Client nods.*] You don't have to make yourself believe him. You don't. And that's okay. It's very frustrating for you, right?

Client: [*nods*] Yeah.

Therapist: 'Cause you don't get all he's feeling, but . . . that's where you are.

Client: Yeah. [*Client and therapist nod.*]

Therapist: How's that to hear?

Client: Good. So then my question is . . .

[*Diana talks while therapy tape is rolling. "Good, but . . ."*]

[*Michael talks while therapy tape is rolling: "Right."*]

Client: How do I not be frustrated when I feel like—or not try to—I guess that's the thing, is, I'm . . . still, I don't agree on his recollection or his story of what happened, and I don't know . . . right now, anyway—maybe later I will because I won't care as much, but I don't know how to be okay with the fact that he has a different story than me. I feel I have to either not care . . .

[*Diana talks while therapy tape is rolling: "Can we stop for a second?"*] [*Michael responds: "Sure."*]

In this vignette, we see in the therapy a parallel process that happened in the supervision session a bit earlier. The client's trust deepens as her sense of shame and unworthiness is undone. She feels she is deserving of good things. She is validated by her therapist, who says, "Of course you want to understand this." Then the client takes a risk and reaches out to the therapist for help. In the supervision vignette that follows, the supervisor uses her experience of the client and makes the implicit explicit of what she is seeing in an AEDP-informed fashion.

SUPERVISION POSTTHERAPY VIGNETTE 8

Diana: I'm very touched by this, because she's actually reaching out to you.

Michael: Mmm. [*nods*]

Diana: She's saying, "I really need help with this." [**supervisor doubling for the client's voice as a way of elaborating the client's experience to help supervisee get what's going on in a deeper way**]

Michael: Mmm. Yeah, yeah.

Diana: You know, again, there's, um . . . and she's honest [**marks transformance manifestation**], so I'm also appreciating *her*. . . . We've talked more about her dysregulation, but she has tremendous strength. [**Supervisor voices the client, that is, narrates her own experience of the supervisee's client.**] [*Michael: "Mmm."*] You know, that's the transformance side of things. [*Michael: "Right. Right."*] That she's really working with you. [*Michael: "Mmm."*] You know, and she's being very honest. [**teaching transformance detection**] [*Michael: "Right. Right."*] So when you—I don't even remember at this point where we came in, and then it was an affirmation, and then she says, "I don't know if I believe you." [*Michael:* "*Right. Right.*"] She's honest. And she's saying, "Tell me more." And you *do* tell her more. Right? [*Michael:* "*Right. Yeah.*"] And now, at this point, she's basically saying, "Help me." [**Supervisor voices the client and narrates her own experience of the client as a way of teaching, making explicit what she sees from a deeply AEDP-informed perspective.**] [*Michael:* "*Yeah.*"] Which is very direct. [*Michael:* "*Yeah. Yeah.*"] But it's connected.

Michael: I can feel the feeling when she was asking, and I was sort of getting this . . . squirmy feeling? [**change moment in the supervision**]

The supervisor's extensive elaboration of the client's experience helps the supervisee viscerally access an experience he had in the therapy session that he hadn't consciously remembered. This represents a moment of experiential deepening in the supervision, one which bespeaks the relational security cocreated: Once again, the supervisee now is willing to let his own direct and quite uncomfortable experience come forth— organized around his feeling "squirmy."

Diana: Uh-huh.

Michael: And also I'm feeling, "Yeah, she's asking a lot of me," and "Can I answer this or can I not?"

Diana: A feeling inside of you.

Michael: Yeah, yeah, just in terms of "how am I gonna handle this? How can I respond? *Can* I respond?"

Be careful what you wish for. AEDP is an attachment-based relational approach, and when relational experiences deepen in our clients, they also touch our own deeper attachment yearnings and insecurities. Here, the client's deepening trust in the therapist emboldens the client to take a risk. Allowing herself to rely on her therapist ups the relational ante and creates anxiety in her therapist. It leads him to wonder whether he is up to the challenge. Note also how the supervisor's doubling for the client, a more right-brained intervention, leads to a deepening of visceral experience for the supervisee, that is, the "squirmy" feeling. In turn, the feeling leads to his viscerally remembering how he had felt in the session.

Michael: I don't wanna, you know, "solve her problems" at all. [*Diana: "Right."*] I'm trying to help her find these—help her think through it, and feel through what she's dealing with. [*Diana: "Right."*] But there is that relational piece that's direct, which I wasn't really conscious of before, or aware of, but yeah . . . [**self-disclosure, green signal affects, which are the equivalent of the green "go" traffic signal light in relationships**]

Diana: Let's do just one more round . . . you know, 'cause it puts a pressure on you, right? It's "Help me! What do I do about this?"

Michael: Right, right, right, yeah. Before, I got the anxiety; now, I'm getting the "that's really good!" [*smiles*] "That's a really good sign!" [**This is a change moment in the supervision; transformation in the here-and-now, a moment of not only "I get it" but "I get it and, whereas I was anxious before, I am happy now." "I feel good now, and my anxiety is gone."**] [*Diana: "Right."*] 'Cause I feel really connected to her, but this is helping me understand *why*, and what that connection's about. [*Diana nods.*] [**Right-brain experience and left-brain understanding are now coming together and getting integrated—and that feels good.**]

Diana: Right. You know that she's trusting you. [*Michael: "Yeah."*] And in a way, it's a very trusting thing to have her say, "I don't know if I believe you." Right? [*Michael: "Right."*] Rather than just, "Yeah, it's great."

Michael: Right. Right. Right. Yeah. Yeah, that's good sign.

Diana: Again, let's just track what's going on with you before we go back.

Michael: It's just feeling good that she can, say, "I don't know." It helps me trust her. When she does say she feels good, then it's, "okay," 'cause she can also say, "I don't know." [**The supervisee is having a deeper appreciation of his client's striving for transformation and its manifestation in personal qualities. As he understands his client better, his trust in her grows.**]

Diana: Exactly. Exactly. She shows her range and her discernment, right? She's not just pleasing you. She's really for real. [*Michael:* "Yeah. Yeah."] I appreciate her. [**elaboration and ongoing articulation of the client's experience, dynamics, personal qualities, transformation manifestations**]

Michael: Me, too.

THERAPY VIGNETTE 9

Client: . . . that his version of history is different from mine, or I have to try to change his version of history [*smiles*], which I can't do—in the same way that I won't let him change mine.

Therapist: Right.

Client: But then I'm also, like, I can't . . . I don't know how to get the answers that I want—I'm not gonna get the answers that I want. [**change moment in the therapy**]

Therapist: Yeah. [*nods*]

Client: [*shakes head, smiles*] Aaah! [*chuckles*]

Therapist: Yeah, that "Aaah." What's that?

Client: [*smiles, twirls her finger around repeatedly*] It just, this all leads back to the same. [*chuckles*]

Therapist: Right, so, so, feelings are gonna come up because you guys are not gonna be able to come together on this. [*shaking head*]

Client: [*nods*] Yeah.

Therapist: Probably. So then lots of feelings are gonna come up. And eventually you're gonna have to accept that's the situation. Right?

Client: [*nods*] Yeah.

Therapist: It's not changing you, it's not changing him, processing all those feelings because of that . . . difference. That really horrible difference, right . . .

Client: [*nods*] Yeah.

Therapist: That's really damaged your life.

Client: Yeah.

Therapist: Right?

Client: Yeah. [*nods*]

Therapist: And, through processing those feelings, eventually you'll come to some acceptance—and not to like it at all.

Client: Yeah.

Therapist: Or agree with it.

Client: Yeah, but just . . . realize it.

Therapist: Yeah, what's resonating with you right now . . .

Client: [*smiles*] But there is a way out. [*laughs*] [**change moment in the therapy**]

Therapist: Yeah. Yeah, definitely. [*smiles*]

Client: [*laughs, then starts to cry*]

Client: It feels good, but it also makes me really, really sad. [**change moment in the therapy**]

Michael: Yeah.

SUPERVISION, POSTTHERAPY VIGNETTE 9

Diana: That's great. In a way, maybe stopping here is even better.

Michael: Yeah.

Diana: We learn about what she was really afraid of once it's lifted, when she says, "There's a way out." Clearly [before], she was feeling, "I will feel this way for eternity [there is no way out]" right? [*Michael:* "Yeah, yeah."] Which is what people feel, one of their pathogenic affects: This is like being in hell and I'm never gonna get out of this hell. [*Michael:* "Yeah.

Yeah. Right."] And, she says, "Oh, there's a way out," which, again, I think is very validating. Now that it is like the true validation; she sort of drops down into the sadness.

Michael: Into the sadness; yeah.

Diana: In terms of the states, and the triangle, how would you track this?

Having come to a place of some closure and a solid experientially based understanding, we now can bring in the left brain to deepen the integration. Once the deep understanding is established, we can translate back and forth between experience (i.e., the experience of the supervision session and understanding one's client and one's own actions better) and reflection (i.e., the theory), which, with new experience, will be deepened.

Michael: I think I was doing a lot of top of the triangle work, State 1 work, and working with anxiety or the defenses. And then through the validation and stuff, and psycho-ed. I think that her having hope was sort of a transformative affect. There was a glimmer of, "Oh, okay, there's a way out." Right?

Diana: More than a glimmer, by the way.

Michael: Yeah. Yeah. And that allowed her to drop into State 2, into the core affect of sadness. You know, we'll see how long [*gestures to TV*], but . . .

Diana: But, look. What occurred to me, now that you were talking, is that she didn't [explicitly] express hopelessness [before]. You know, hopelessness that she would ever be out of purgatory . . . [*Michael: "Right."*] So I think it's an adaptive action tendency of the pathogenic affect. It's not helpless, it's not hopeless; it's gonna be okay. [*Michael: "Right."*] Or, not okay, but "I'm gonna get out of it." [*Michael: "Yeah."*] "I'm gonna get out of it." And then that lets her drop down into core affect.

Michael: Yeah, yeah, yeah.

Diana: Sorry to rush us, but we don't have a lot of time left. Are we—is there another . . . are we? [**As the attachment figure, it is the job of the**

supervisor to track time and other boundary issues that help create a good container for the work.]

Michael: There is a little metaprocessing at the end. We can skip to that.

Diana: Great. Okay. So let's watch the last couple of minutes of the session here.

THERAPY VIGNETTE 10

Therapist: So, how are you doing right now? How's this?

Client: [*smiles*] Good. [*chuckles*] It was good. [**transformational affect—declarative**] I liked your talking more, instead of me just spewing at you for an hour. [*laughs*]

Therapist: [*smiles*] Yeah. Previously, you seemed like the emotion was bigger? Right?

Client: Too much, yeah. [*laughs*]

Therapist: Is that your sense?

Client: Yeah, it's more manageable. [*chuckles*] [**explicit assertion of transformation**]

Therapist: Yeah, more of a conversation.

Client: Yeah. [*nods*] Yeah. And . . . Yes. [*sighs, pauses*] There will be a way out of this. [*chuckles*] [**change moment in the therapy**] I guess it just seems more visible now than it did before. [**explicit assertion of transformation**]

Therapist: How does that feel?

Client: Good, actually. I think, too, having conversations with, you know, different people, and I wasn't ready for people to say, "You'll be fine down the road. You'll find someone else" I'm like, "I am so not ready for that yet!" And I'm still not, but I'm a lot closer to it. [**assertion of transformation**]

Therapist: It's okay to be right where you are. You had the sense that it will be okay at some point, but right now it's not, and that's okay. Right, that's okay to be here right now.

Client: [*nods*] Mmm. Yes. [**change moment in the therapy**] [*takes deep breath*] [**positive somatic–affective transformational marker**]

Therapist: [*smiles*] Big sigh. [**moment-to-moment tracking of somatic marker**]

Client: [*chuckles*] Yeah. It's okay. [**assertion of transformation**]

Therapist: Well, I appreciate you sharing all of this with me, and just being vulnerable, and just sharing feelings. How's that to hear?

Client: Thank you. [*smiles*] This is good. [**explicit assertion of transformation**]

SUPERVISION, POSTTHERAPY VIGNETTE 10

Diana: Great. Great. Just if we're tracking here, how might you describe what's happening? Sort of from phenomenology . . . [**asking supervisee to reflect on how his experience of the session can be understood in the terms of AEDP theory, which, given his visceral experience of transformation in the session, will be deepened**]

Michael: We're metaprocessing the session. [*Diana: "Right."*] And then she's—you know, in reflecting on it, I think, she comes to some temporarily stable position in which I think there's elements of, um, a core state. [*Diana: "Yeah."*] Calmness, and there's an openness, and sort of a kindness towards herself that wasn't there before.

Diana: That's right.

Michael: And then, my validation, I think, of that, then we start going back up [*chuckles*] to State 2, so the sadness then comes up just momentarily, but, um . . .

Diana: The sadness.

Michael: Yeah, there was a little bit, I forget what—I do some validation and stuff that helps her reflect on where she is, and then some of her sadness comes up a little bit at the end. [*Diana:* "Right. Right."] Right, there's the State 4 and then going back up to State 2 a little bit.

Diana: A little bit. I think what was also very significant is that she tells us that the process is regulatory for her—that the emotion that was so big and overwhelming is now . . . I think she uses the word *manageable.* [*Michael:* "Right."] And I was looking at her very, very closely, and she starts to have a real direct gaze, real direct contact with you, when she's talking about that. And the entry point I wrote here, "sunshine," you know, she has such a nice smile, and, again, she says, "There will be a way out," which is a huge, huge thing for her. [**The supervisor is heightening the importance of the client's transformational affects, that is, the positive somatic–affective evidence of the transformation occurring.**] [*Michael:* "Yeah."] And again, her connection with you is beautiful. [**deeply felt affirmation**] [*Michael:* "Mmm."] When you say, "So what's it like for you?" and she says, "Okay," and again, it's real, 'cause she's honest. [*Michael:* "Right."] And then, if you had any doubts, you get the sigh.

Michael: [*chuckles*] Right. [**positive somatic–affective transformational marker**]

Diana: The nervous system checks in and says [*sighs*], and I have the sense that if you were to track the amount of anxiety and shame at the beginning, and where we are now, she's got an answer. I sort of want to know, where are *you* vis-à-vis *your* questions? I mean, your questions are explicit, we didn't know she had a question, but we discovered she had a question. [**Now, with a lot of experience and understanding under their belts, the supervisor and supervisee go back to his original questions, which shaped their supervision session, for one last round of integration of right-brain experience and left-brained understanding.**]

The supervisor and the supervisee are cocreating a coherent and cohesive narrative of the therapy session. This cocreation includes an understanding of the client and the therapist's deepened understanding of himself and his therapeutic interventions in the context of a supportive, affirming supervisory relationship. With that comes a deepened understanding of AEDP theory and phenomenology from the point of view of direct felt experience in the context of the supervisory dyad.

Michael: [*chuckles*] I feel good about the advocacy I did on her behalf and with her, because the way she ends up, and my checking in with her. I think that was good. That worked. That was effective. [*chuckles*] [**change moment in the supervision, evidence of transformation**]

Diana: How do you feel about that? [**metaprocessing transformational experience**]

Michael: I feel good about that. Yeah. Yeah.

Diana: Could you tell me just a bit more about that?

Michael: Yeah, 'cause, I mean, when I was doing it, I was [thinking], "Is this too much?" I felt I was really meeting her in a really strong, engaged way.

Diana: Mmm. Yeah.

It is wonderful to see the supervisee's precise positive evaluation of his own self, which will deeply support his positive identity as a therapist and provide fuel and motivation for further growth and development as a therapist, and as an AEDP therapist.

Michael: Which she mentions, you know, says that she liked me talking more—I think that's what she meant, I was really active with her, and it feels really good to have that work, and I can see that that worked. I'm evaluating, it's a feeling of "I can do that." I can be that way in session with clients, and, you know, check in with them, and if it works, if the client gets—makes progress [*they chuckle*]—then I can do that, it feels good. [**change moment in the supervision**] I feel I added and have expanded as a therapist, or grown as a therapist. [**broaden-and-build aspects of meta-therapeutic processing in terms of the self-experience and supervisee's identity as a therapist**]

This is a huge moment of transformation—the culmination of the supervisory process. It thus is important to further metaprocess this moment to make the most of the opportunity here. Let's deepen it, consolidate it, and expand it through some more metaprocessing.

Diana: Ah! Stay with that for a moment, the sense of expanding as a therapist. [**notice and seize, and stay!**]

Michael: I feel bigger. [**change moment in the supervision**] [*chuckles*] [**assertion of transformation**] [*Diana: "Uh-huh."*] I notice myself breathing, better, fuller. Yeah. [**transformational affects**]

Diana: You know, and as you're saying that, I notice myself getting very happy. [**transformational affects for supervisor, self-disclosure of effect of supervisee on supervisor**] It's such a lovely thing to—I was gonna say witness, but really, to be part of . . . you know, just starting with a question, but it's also a self-doubt, not a pathological one, the . . . you know, we all have self—"Am I doing the right thing? Is this too much? Too little?" [*Michael: "Right."*] And to end in a place of feeling validated, but also expanded. [*Michael: "Yeah."*] That seems pretty good! [**change moment in the supervision**]

Michael: Yeah, it feels good.

Diana: [*Raises hand for a high-five.*] So I wanna say, all right!

Michael: All right! [*They high-five and laugh.*]

Energized is a key quality of supervision that is transformative (Watkins, 2012). In the last minutes of the supervision, we see a positive upward transformational spiral in action. The supervision ends with a deep resonance and a sense that both participants have been transformed. Just as the supervisee feels good and has an expanded—and growing—sense of himself and an experience of satisfaction and pride in his competence because he helped his client, so does the supervisor. She has an experience of satisfaction, pride, and happiness, as a result of having helped her supervisee. The mission was accomplished, and it is apt that this supervision session ends in a moment of affective affirmation, experiencing, and resonance of mission accomplished, well done, and the high spirits—the high-five—that come with it.

CONCLUSION

We end Chapter 3 with the exuberance of a high-five. Chapter 4 will guide you explicitly through some of the practical issues you have just experienced behind the scenes: spending time at the beginning of the meeting to understand and help organize the supervisee's specific questions, learning how to use video recording for supervision and how we use descriptive rather than evaluative interventions, and discovering how the AEDP Fidelity Scale (Faerstein & Levenson, 2016) keeps us all on track.

4

Practical Issues

Time taken at the beginning of a supervisory relationship to set the frame and be clear about expectations is time extremely well spent. The clear communication of how supervision works best helps both supervisor and supervisee: The clearer the frame, the clearer the expectations, the more productive the sessions. The first conversations are of utmost importance, as are the first minutes of each supervisory session; the supervisor must set the stage. We, the supervisors, move more slowly as we set the frame. The essential skill of slowing down—"Let's slow down, let's really take our time here, would that be all right?"—helps us create space to be clear about how supervision works best.

The same question that accelerated experiential dynamic psychotherapy (AEDP) uses—"What is it specifically that I can help you with?"—is reflected in the supervisory session when we ask, "How can I be helpful?"— namely, "What is it specifically that you would like me to see in your video?"

http://dx.doi.org/10.1037/0000016-005
Supervision Essentials for Accelerated Experiential Dynamic Psychotherapy, by N. C. N. Prenn and D. Fosha

"What are you working on?" "What are your client's stated goals?" The supervision session should address these intersecting questions. The issue or question may be about a particular place where a supervisee notices he or she gets stuck or doesn't know what to do next. With the question in hand, the texture and fabric of the supervisory session are coconstructed with what the supervisee and the client bring into the session, and how the supervisor responds.

THE CENTRALITY OF VIDEO RECORDING
TO THE AEDP SUPERVISORY PROCESS

The AEDP supervisory process relies almost exclusively on video recordings of clinical work. Supervisors privilege and value the moment-to-moment microanalysis of the physical, emotional, and cognitive experience of therapist and client. This focus on the here-and-now interactions between client and therapist, and the shared discussion of the therapist–client interaction with their supervisors has proven to be an effective way to teach psychotherapists how to improve their psychotherapy. Given the emphasis in the research literature of accountability (Watkins, 2012) and immediate feedback (Goodyear & Nelson, 1997), the importance of doing supervision from actual videos of the therapy session cannot be overstated.

Videorecording is an essential part of the supervision process for three reasons (Sarnat, 2012; Watkins, 2012):

- It provides an accurate and reliable record of the session rather than relying on memory and imagination.
- The process of watching the tape is experiential, allowing the supervisee to experience and share in the supervisor's experiential and visceral responses.
- Supervisees learn a tremendous amount from viewing and rating their videos with the AEDP Fidelity Scale (AEDP-FS; Faerstein & Levenson, 2016; see Chapter 7, this volume). Watching their videos is how therapists can self-monitor. The reviewing of videos after a session is a way for therapists to check their work for themselves.

Technology

One of the first tasks an AEDP supervisee must master is technological: What kind of camera or computer will work best in his or her office? How will a supervisee transfer the video from camera to portable drive or memory card that will work with the supervisor's computer or TV? For most therapists (i.e., supervisors and supervisees), this second area of expertise is a challenge—one that they need active help with. Once the equipment is in place, supervisees need to generate a personalized permission form to videorecord their clients; then, they need to ask permission from their clients. This is an area of anxiety for most therapists: introducing their own need into the relationship with a client. Whom to ask first, how to ask, and how to manage their own anxiety and need are focuses of initial supervisory sessions.

The Skill of Watching Video Recordings

Before showing the video, the supervisor asks the supervisee questions like: "How can I help?" "What are you wanting me to notice?" "What are we going to see?" "What do you want us to focus on?" "How do you feel about this piece of work? If you feel proud, what specifically are you pleased that you did? If embarrassed or concerned, what specifically did you do or say or not do and not say that concerns you?" "How many minutes of video are you hoping to watch with me?"

Next, we ask supervisees (and workshop participants) to notice their method of watching video. "How do you watch the recording?" "Do you identify with the client?" "Do you identify with the therapist?" "Do you merge and become porous to the material and affect? If so, what is this like as an experience?" "Do you get activated and space out?" "Does a critical part of you come up?"

Documentation: "Existing in Our Heart and Mind"

In the same way that supervisors try to show up authentically with our supervisees, it is important to be the rememberer of their therapy sessions. We all have a need to be known and recognized, and to be memorable—to have an effect on another person and know that we have (Fosha, 2009a). The video is enormously helpful in this regard. We can see, hear, and feel our supervisees' clients, and so we have many ways to remember them. When we do remember and we say, "Yes, I have seen Jim before. I remember him," we let our supervisees know that we hold them in our heart and mind (Fosha, 2000b). This is a good opportunity to make this remembering explicit and to metaprocess: "How is it for you that I remember Jim?"

In addition to recording our supervision sessions, supervisors keep notes to document the clients in our supervisees' care and to document what each supervisee is working on. We keep track of their knowledge of AEDP, their intrapsychic and interpersonal capacities, and the specific skills we have encouraged them to practice week to week. Our notes include our coconstructed ideas about the learning edge of each supervisee. As you might imagine, this documentation is part of an ongoing collaborative process. Everything is talked about explicitly and metaprocessed so that we are cocreating the learning experience together.

What is different about AEDP documentation is that the supervisor's focus is more on the experience and dynamics than on content or history (although, over time, supervisors learn about life events if we follow one client closely because we do ask for the context of the session we are about to watch). *Experiential dynamic* means just that: Through the experience moment-to-moment in session, the dynamics will shine through and the history will reveal itself, as necessary. This is also where the AEDP schemas help us: We draw the triangle of experience in our notes every session. "What is the client's core emotion in this moment, in this session?" "What are her favorite protective strategies (defenses)?" "How does she experience anxiety?"

EVALUATION/DESCRIPTION

The word *evaluation* holds an anticipation of criticism and judgment. When we substitute the word *description* in its place, we are more aligned with our way of working in AEDP supervision. This means there is no single, separate, summative year-end evaluation but, rather, a continuous formative learning process that evolves via metaprocessing and moment-to-moment tracking. AEDP supervision is a process-oriented, process-tracking process. It has no performance evaluations, but supervisors consistently check in about the learning process and how it is working for both participants.

Supervisors lead with all we see, feel, hear, and notice. We are modeling our moment-to-moment tracking skills. Gradually, we add other ideas and tools to the supervisory space. The supervisor asks the supervisee, "Would it be okay with you right now if I said a couple of things that come to my mind as we look at this together?"

The supervisor describes what she is experiencing about what the supervisee has done in a session with the client: "This is what I am seeing." "This is what I am imagining." "At this moment, if we stop the video recording, I am wondering . . ." In this way, we add a third subjectivity to an ongoing dyadic subjectivity: We lend our minds, our expertise, and our way of thinking to our supervisees in a "gradual, non-traumatic" way (Bollas, 1987, p. 208). This narrating, platforming, musing aloud, and describing our inner response to the case material lends itself to a playful experience with the clinical work because the supervisor's imaginings open a pathway to inviting the supervisee to join in the wondering about what he or she was thinking, feeling, seeing, and hearing in the session (or in the current supervisory meeting). The spirit of wondering—of curiosity and joint discovery—creates an open-to-learning state: A supervisee recently said to the supervisor (i.e., Prenn), "I don't have to defend against your supervisory remarks." The supervisor is not the expert and does not position him- or herself in that way.

Christopher Bollas (1987) wrote of Winnicott that it was his attitude toward his own thought processes that made communication nonintrusive and nontraumatic to his clients. Thoughts were meant "to be played with—kicked around, mulled over, torn to pieces, rather than regarded as the official version of the truth" (Bollas, 1987, p. 206). This putting of ideas out into the facilitating environment of the supervisory session with tentativeness and in a spirit of play is part of the essence of AEDP supervision. In AEDP, supervisors announce our subjectivity by using *I* statements;

we make clear that this is an idea, not the final authoritarian conceptualization. The client–therapist dyad has its own rhythm and pace; it is important that the supervisory session augment the dyad's repertoire of interactions and not intrude on it or disrupt it too much.

Expanding on the work of Bollas, we offer more supervisory interventions: "I am thinking that," "I have an idea," "what occurs to me is," and "I sense you move away." As supervisors, we announce our ability to play with supervisory interventions by starting to say something and course-correcting as we speak (an intervention that the supervisor, i.e., Prenn, calls the *interruption*): "This is what I am seeing and feeling as I watch your client . . . Wait! Let me check in with myself—although plausible, that doesn't seem quite right. Let me stop and try again" (Bollas, 1987, pp. 206–207). Another nonintrusive way of expanding or stretching a supervisee's repertoire of interventions might go something like this: "Notice what you did: You intervened in this way here and your client responded with relaxation and deep eye contact, great! I like what you did, and what else might you have said and done?"

Supervisee says, "I might have asked, 'I would like to slow us down right here.'"

Supervisor: "Yes. That is a good idea. I like that. How else could you intervene around slowing down? Would it be okay with you if we made a list of slowing down interventions?"

If a supervisee makes what a supervisor considers a mistake, it creates safety when supervisors judiciously and tactfully say what we think, and the client reaction confirms that the therapist made a mistake. Limiting our feedback to praise only ultimately does not create safety. We often say in AEDP that there are no mistakes—only what you do next: metaprocess. In a recent core training, a supervisee showed a video of a moving change moment with a client. At the end of the session, while metaprocessing the change moment, the therapist–supervisee made a general comment about her work with other clients. This explicit referencing of other clients led her client to cross her arms, tear up, and break eye contact. The therapist did not notice this reaction at the time, but now watching the recording, she clearly saw that the client had a strong reaction. In response, the supervisor said she thought talking about other clients in general is a mistake.

The supervisee agreed and felt encouraged that she now knew not to do that in the future; she also felt encouraged to try to bring the matter up with her client at the next meeting. Incidentally, this exchange occurred in a group setting of core training with 10 other therapists. It was a good way to teach the group a general rule, and the supervisor felt there was enough group safety and vulnerability among all the participants to say directly that she thought this was a mistake. The client's reaction was the strongest guide of all.

Rigor Without Shame: Self-Supervision and the AEDP Fidelity Scale

As supervisees move toward certification in AEDP, they must follow specific guidelines. This expectation is made explicit throughout the process, so there are no surprises. The AEDP-FS (see https://www.aedpinstitute. org/wp-content/uploads/2014/01/AEDP-Fidelity-Scale-Self-Report.pdf) and self-supervision handouts sharpen the growing edges of learning. The AEDP-FS (Faerstein & Levenson, 2016), developed by Levenson and the AEDP Institute faculty, measures not only whether a therapist is using a particular skill but also how well he or she is demonstrating the skill. The self-supervision handouts we have developed list the skills that supervisees need to be able to demonstrate to be considered AEDP practitioners. They are concrete and, thus, tend to reduce anxiety.

Using these evaluative tools, supervisors can rate videotaped segments to quantify what supervisees are doing; we can also flag interventions and capacities that are areas to develop over time. It is an opportunity for the supervisee's own reflection and own self-assessment, and a further opportunity to learn more deeply about the aspects of AEDP. Using the AEDP-FS to rate clinical work is another way for supervisees to internalize the process, learn, get better, appreciate areas of competence, and be motivated to expand that competence into areas that need further development, work, and practice. The supervisor provides support and scaffolding, too.

One good way to track supervisees that supervisors find particularly useful and nonshaming is the use of specific interventions. To this end, we use intervention handouts that catalogue specific skill headings and interventions to use. The interventions are the recognizable bones and structure of AEDP, and easy to identify as the video is playing. Supervisors say things like: "Look at your affirming, your delighting, your defense recognition, your moment-to-moment tracking." The most challenging interventions tend to be around the relationship and relatedness, particularly around receiving thanks and gratitude from the supervisee or client. We have been trained in other therapies not to explore the experience of the positive in the relationship. A thank you has been thought to be enough (Hanakawa, 2011). In AEDP, it isn't: It is an entry point into an exploration. Our ability to receive and express our pleasure and pride in the relationship and in the client's progress is a healing experience in and of itself: We model it in supervision and we practice it in our AEDP therapy sessions.

Here is a list of AEDP techniques and interventions:

- Slow down: "Let's slow down."
- Notice affect-laden/feeling words and explore: "What's that sadness like?"
- Orient client to internal experience: "I wonder what you are experiencing inside?"
- Moment-to-moment tracking of experience and relatedness: "You lean forward as you tell me that."
- Notice and seize an entry point, and intervene: "Something comes up here."
- Remember to metaprocess throughout: "How are we doing?"
- Affirm: "That is right! You are doing great!"
- Ask permission: "Would it be okay if we stayed with this for a minute?" (Include a time limit.)
- Invite to collaborate: "Can we . . . ?"
- Include the body: "What are you experiencing inside as you are talking?"
- Moment-to-moment tracking: "A smile! A frown! A tear! A sigh!"
- Metaprocess/make explicit relationship: "How is it that I see . . . that I notice . . . that I care?"
- Self-disclose the effect of the client on you: "I am moved; I appreciate; wow, I am touched by how you x, y, z."

Small Group Supervision

Group supervision is a popular format for AEDP supervision. Group members learn from and support each other in their learning. Two formats work well. Where homogeneity exists in terms of level of AEDP training, we form a group in which all members are at about the same level of AEDP proficiency. The second type of group borrows from Montessori mixed-age groupings in that we have group members at different levels of training; we learn from those more advanced than we are and also learn by seeing what we already know well. Although we concentrate a lot on what happens in the supervision group meeting itself, a lot of metaprocessing and preanxiety regulating happens in walks to the subway, carpools, and rides in elevators. Asking more experienced group members to explicitly welcome and help their fellow group members leads to more safety and integration.

Vignette: You Will Think: "How Can This Anxious Mess Help This Anxious Client?"

The setting is a small group. We meet twice a month for 2 hours. One of the group members, Jacky, begins:

> I am not usually anxious coming in to show videotape anymore, but for some reason, I had a real shame spiral last night and now again this morning. I felt . . . I feel anxious and inadequate. I feel so embarrassed. I am going to show you a segment of a client struggling with anxiety, and I am so anxious. I am afraid that you are going to think, "How can this anxious mess help this anxious client?"

How do I (i.e., Prenn) work as a supervisor here?
The supervisor asks Jacky, "How is it sharing this with us [the group]?"
"It is okay, I guess. I am glad I told you," she says.
"Oh, thank you," another group member says. "I am so glad you are telling us and bringing work that you are really struggling with. I always learn so much when you do that. Thank you! Thank you!"
"How is this to hear?" the supervisor asks. [**metaprocess**]

"It is good and a bit of a relief. I was wondering about parallel process," Jacky says.

"I was wondering about that, too," says the supervisor. "Maybe this anxiety and shame are his, too. He feels so inadequate, and maybe you are holding some of that, really getting that."

"Yes," says Jacky. "That sounds right. Possible."

"How can we help?" the supervisor asks.

"Don't judge me! You will see my foot in the video—it is jiggling like mad. I was anxious in the session. Ugh, I feel so embarrassed, so ashamed. I keep thinking, 'I am such an anxious mess! How can I help him?'"

The supervisor smiles. "A lot of thoughts activating you." She raises her hands to form the triangle of experience. "I wonder where you are?"

"Oh, top-top-top of the triangle!" Jacky says.

"I know," says the supervisor. "Can we get out of your head and feel your body right now?"

Jacky nods and takes a deep breath. "I feel lonely inside as I sit with you."

"Lonely?"

"Like no one knows me," Jacky says. "I am all alone. I am alone. Hidden away."

"That is so important. Let's hold onto that while we watch. Does that sound okay?"

Jacky nods.

We watch the beginning of the session. The client is talking: He is disconnected from feeling. We comment on how fast he is talking and about slowing him down. Jacky, the therapist, says, "I wanted you to see what he was like when he came in. I couldn't get a word in edgewise!"

The supervisor offers a suggestion about slowing down the client, asking him if he can make eye contact with Jacky, his therapist. The client feels alone with himself as he talks about how anxious he feels, how he hates his body, and how he feels unattractive. Jacky moves the video ahead to a segment she has preselected to show what happens when they do slow down a bit. We as a group notice that Jacky has to work hard to intervene. After several attempts, Jacky does succeed in slowing him down quite a bit: "All of this is so important. I want to know all, and right now—phew—let's take a breath together here. Would that be okay?" Jacky says. The client offers a sigh of relief.

"I like what you said," the supervisor says, "and when he said 'relief,' I could see relief in his body as he slowed down, and it seemed like his nervous system regulated at that moment."

"Yes, yes. I see that," Jacky responds.

"And so I wonder if that might have been a place to try to hold him. He started talking again, and I am not sure what happened for him."

A group member reflects on this moment, too. "The client is saying that, and his body is relaxing, and your foot stopped wiggling! You could ask, 'How is your body feeling now? How does it feel inside now?' So he can have that shift and know he has had it, and update his here-and-now experience of himself with you."

"Yes, yes, I know," Jacky says enthusiastically, brightening.

"How was this to share this work with us today?" the supervisor asks. [**metaprocessing**]

"It was good. I feel better," says Jacky.

"I am glad," says the supervisor. "And could I just check in—would that be okay? [**asking permission**] [*Jacky nods.*] How do you know—how do you experience feeling better physically?" [**somatic exploration**]

Jacky sighs.

"A big sigh," the supervisor gently reflects. "Yes, steadier, taller, calmer." Her eyes are clear, her gaze direct.

"Thank you; this feels better," says Jacky. "I was feeling so ashamed and so alone. Phew, this feels better. Phew." She takes in the rest of the group with her eyes. "Wow, thank you all."

Supervision groups can be affectively challenging, particularly when dynamic material is being presented and when a parallel process is in play. Supervisees often bring in clients who are working on the very thing that the supervisee is struggling with: The client who shuts down in session and the supervisee who, unusually, shuts down in the supervisory hour. Another example is the supervisee who rushes from one case to another and doesn't have enough time in the supervisory hour; that supervisee shows a video of a client rushing to tell one story after another and doesn't have enough time in the therapy hour. Or consider the client who is overly complimentary of how much the therapist is helping; now, the supervisee is overly complimentary of his or her supervisor. The video and affect contagion make this phenomenon even more omnipresent.

Over time and as group safety increases, trainees and faculty bring in and show increasingly complicated video clips of how we are all doing the work. We show a mix of excerpts to teach various theoretical constructs and get to know different kinds of scenarios—such as having work not go smoothly or getting stuck—so that trainees feel that learning the model is attainable.

CONCLUSION

In this chapter, we covered practical aspects of AEDP supervision: the centrality of video recordings and how AEDP evaluation is descriptive rather than evaluative. We talked about the AEDP Fidelity Scale and outlined the concrete skills that supervisees need to be able to demonstrate to be considered for AEDP certification. You saw that although AEDP involves affirmation and a positive approach, it also involves specific schemas and skill sets that make the process rigorous and, in many ways, uniform. This rigor allows for supervisees to learn specific skills and interventions, and provides a training that is without shame or surprise. In the next chapter, we talk about working with different attachment styles, the different levels of experience our supervisees come to us with, and how important it is for us as supervisors to be adaptable.

5

Common Challenges

M ost of our supervisees come to us because they want to learn accelerated experiential dynamic psychotherapy (AEDP): They are excited
and motivated, and come of their own volition. They almost always are
ideal supervisees. However, sometimes problems arise, and it's important
to know how to address them. This chapter describes how an AEDP supervisor adapts to work with a range of difficult or challenging supervisees
and supervisory issues.

It has become standard practice in psychotherapy and in psychotherapy supervision to talk about symptoms, psychopathology, difficult clients,
and difficult supervisees. AEDP looks for health and potential: It understands difficult supervisees as living primarily at the top of the triangle in
State 1, anxiety and defense. It also conceptualizes difficulties as being the
best defensive (i.e., adaptive) strategies available to that person at that time.

http://dx.doi.org/10.1037/0000016-006
Supervision Essentials for Accelerated Experiential Dynamic Psychotherapy, by N. C. N. Prenn and
D. Fosha

Through step-by-step, moment-to-moment attunement to the supervisee, the supervisor is creative as he or she tries to adapt to the supervisee. Supervisors try to stay in positively valenced interactions. When we are not in sync or our meetings feel stuck, flat, or unhelpful, we work to get back in sync and to repair and energize the supervision. We work for our supervisees and in the service of their clients. It is our job to put to use our AEDP knowledge, capacities, and skills to be a versatile supervisor. If, as a supervisor, we don't know that our supervisee is not learning or is not engaged, or has difficulties learning from us, then we supervisors have work to do. It is our job to adapt to our supervisees; if they have a hard time learning something, then it is our job to figure out how to teach it to them. As Hanna Levenson (1995) said in *Time-Limited Dynamic Psychotherapy*, "'difficult' clients are not being 'resistant'; they are attempting to do the best they can with how they construe the world, and the therapeutic work is meeting them where they are" (p. 177). This tenet applies to supervision: When supervisees have differences and difficulties, that is the work.

SUPERVISING DIFFERENCES

Supervisees come to supervisors with varying degrees of talent and aptitude for AEDP and therapy; most supervisees are neither highly gifted nor completely devoid of talent. As supervisors, our job is to try to figure out what they do well and help them do more of it. We also work to discover what is getting in the way of their being able to practice AEDP. What are the capacities and skills that they need to develop?

In supervision, supervisees must discuss the most embarrassing and difficult problems with clients, but the harder the issue, the more supervisees need to feel safe bringing it up. When supervision is not going well, supervisees increasingly censor and filter themselves, so it is of paramount importance that we create conditions that are the most conducive to sharing vulnerability. When we look for strength, what is going well, and what is already happening, and celebrate our supervisees, we create conditions of safety and trust. We cocreate energy in the work and keep it feeling lively and vital when we self-disclose that we, too, sometimes don't know what to do; when we get curious with our supervisees about the clients with whom they are having a hard time working (as opposed to focusing on a "difficult" client); and when we undo aloneness and finds ways to get alongside our supervisees.

What are common challenges in supervision, and how can we, as supervisors, adapt?

WORKING WITH DIFFERENT ATTACHMENT STYLES

Supervisees come to AEDP supervision with different attachment styles and internal working models. Some need to put more words to their feelings; others need to put more feelings to their words (Wallin, 2007). Some of us feel and don't deal; others deal and don't feel; and some of us sometimes deal, and sometimes reel, and sometimes feel (Fosha, 2000b). Some are overregulated and love intellectual learning, and need to understand concepts intellectually before they can try something new. Others are in their bodies in the now with their experience and their emotion, and need to learn to have more reflection on what they feel and put theory to their intuitive clinical practice.

In session or in between meetings, supervisors can often be alerted to an anxious or avoidant attachment strategy in our interactions with supervisees. For example, the anxious/preoccupied supervisee perceives an emergency and calls her supervisor: "I just made a mistake in my session, and I don't think my client will come back. What should I do?" Meanwhile, the avoidant, dismissive, self-reliant supervisee hospitalizes a client without even contacting her supervisor! Attachment styles come through defensive strategies (schematically located in State 1 on the triangle of experience). A supervisor can't offer a new interaction or a new experience unless he or she has an idea about the old—the procedural pattern of responding—so it's best to start by gathering information, for instance, by doing or saying something relational and noticing the supervisee's response: a simple "How are we doing? How is this relationship going for you?" or the metaprocessing of an affirmation or a compliment: "How is it for you to have me compliment your work with this client?"

ACCELERATED EXPERIENTIAL DYNAMIC PSYCHOTHERAPY SUPERVISION

Preoccupied/Anxious Attachment: Feel and Reel

The strategies/defenses of preoccupied/anxious supervisees (top of the triangle—see Figure 1.2) tend to present in an overactivation. They often have many compelling stories to tell, jump from client to client and topic to topic, and complain about others. They are "other" focused: The other is the solution and their perceived source of comfort.

As a result, they can feel in need of reassurance and comforting words and advice. They often attack themselves: "I am a terrible therapist," "I shouldn't even be a therapist," "this is hopeless—I'll never get this." Their thoughts and words often drive up their levels of activation and up-regulate their states of arousal and emotion. These are their anxiety and defense mechanisms. Such supervisees need more internal capacity: They need more ability to reflect on what they are feeling internally. Meta-processing and reflecting together build more ability to reflect and put words to feelings, and, ultimately, distinguish anxiety from feeling. It can be helpful to say to anxious/preoccupied supervisees "let's slow down and take a breath" or "let's take our time at the beginning of our meeting," while assuring him or her that you, the supervisor, will still get to everything that is important.

Avoidant/Dismissive: Deal and Don't Feel

The strategies/defenses of avoidant/dismissive supervisees (top of the triangle) tend to present as underactivation. These supervisees intellectualize, minimize, deny needs, and are overly self-reliant. The work to expand the overregulated supervisee is in self-other strategies. This supervisee may need encouragement to ask for help and to connect to his or her feelings inside and to others interpersonally.

Disorganized Attachment: Feel and Sometimes Reel and Sometimes Deal

A disorganized attachment style is the most challenging to work with—as a therapist or a supervisor. Disorganized attachment strategies stem from caregivers who are at one and the same time the object of comfort and source of fear. Toddlers approach frightening caregivers with arms outstretched and faces turned away: They need and they fear. This approach/ avoid strategy calls for creativity and sensitivity on the part of the supervisor. If you are feeling confused by your supervisee, who sometimes urgently needs your help and, at other times, is surprised that you offer your availability, be on the alert that your supervisee may have different "parts" of him or her coming to supervision. *Parts language* is a good way to introduce conflicting and, at times, opposing needs: "Part of you can take care of this and feels confident. Perhaps other parts have other ideas. How do you think you will feel when you are back in your office with this client?"

SKILL DEFICIT/TRAINEE IMPAIRMENT

Skill deficit and trainee impairment address two different areas of expertise: The first comprises the building blocks of the therapy; the second speaks to the trainee's capacities. Most AEDP supervisees come for supervision because they want to learn AEDP skills. They know they are skill deficient, and supervisors start to build the blocks of AEDP therapy from there. Trainee impairment is sometimes less easy to identify. Often, one has a sense of something getting in the way. We can intuit that it has to do with their relationship with themselves or others. Often, supervisees drawn to AEDP want to be more relational in their therapy relationships and in their personal lives, too. Relational interventions (see Chapter 2) can be most challenging for supervisees who have been trained in treatment modalities that used an internal focus or the therapeutic relationship in less overt or explicit ways.

The inability to reliably use particular skills with clients may relate to trainee impairment in some way. Therapists often have experiential dynamic blocks that prevent them from intervening in a particular way, and if supervisors gently inquire, we often quickly find out the reason why. Knowing why in our prefrontal cortex does not necessarily mean we can change something in practice, but often just starting to unpack the difficulties loosens something up, and change can begin. We try to give our supervisees recursive experiences of what they are trying to learn as therapists, as it is in embodied experiences that deep and lasting change occurs.

Are there therapists who simply cannot learn AEDP? Here, the video recordings are essential: We can see together how a client reacts to everything a therapist does or doesn't do verbally and nonverbally. We can see where a therapist talks too much or not enough. We can start there and then simply invite a supervisee to try to slow a client down or notice an affect-laden word. We have not had the experience that a supervisee cannot learn AEDP.

ADAPT TO THE AEDP EXPERIENCE LEVEL OF YOUR SUPERVISEE

Supervisors identify the supervisee's current level of familiarity with AEDP and provide supervision appropriate to where they are, while simultaneously facilitating the movement of supervisee to the next level. A beginner therapist and a more experienced therapist will need different kinds of intervention, structure, and help. AEDP is not, strictly speaking, a levels or stages model of supervision, but we pay attention to how much time on task an AEDP therapist–supervisee has when we begin work together.

McNeill and Stoltenberg (2016; in this Clinical Supervision Essentials Series) developed the integrated developmental model of supervision to explain the stages a trainee goes through as he or she gains confidence as a therapist and how supervisors can aid that development. In their model, trainees pass through three developmental levels, and as they gain experience, structured supervision decreases. It is helpful to think about these stages and how they can apply to learning and teaching AEDP. Preliminary research has indicated that a number of AEDP's skills and tenets enable AEDP therapists to progress through different stages at an accelerated pace (Iwakabe, Fosha, & Edlin, 2016; see Chapter 7, this volume, p. 153).

Although a levels approach sounds linear, in practice it is not. It is dyadic and dynamic. A particular supervisee may feel deskilled or experience a high level of anxiety when faced with a particular client or client situation. Regardless of level, the skills and interventions that are the backbone and structure of AEDP remain the same. The goals of treatment and, therefore, what we are hoping to see in our supervisees' sessions are the same.

This idea of levels or phases of development extends to supervisors, as well: A beginning supervisor will need more specific structural help, particularly around "frame" issues, than a more experienced supervisor. We say more about frame issues in Chapter 6 when we discuss ongoing training for supervisors.

SENIORITY OF TRAINEES

Because AEDP attracts so many therapists who are already established, it is relatively common for an AEDP supervisor to train and supervise a more seasoned therapist–trainee. In such circumstances, it's easy for a supervisor to wonder, "What can I possibly teach him or her?" However when we see how working experientially and relationally is different for a lot of therapists, we can relax and see that we can teach our trainee AEDP, even though he or she has 20 or 30 years of experience as a psychotherapist.

Incorporating AEDP into what experienced trainees already may know poses particular challenges. It can be difficult to feel like a beginner again when one has been practicing psychotherapy successfully for years. This is different from working with therapists who are just out of school or newly in practice. Learning AEDP can provoke defenses related to one's personal history or to giving up or modifying the approaches the supervisee used before AEDP. All learning requires receptivity and, as supervisors, we must help supervisees be alert to defenses to ward off shame and criticism (M. Fried, personal communication, March 21, 2016). Nonjudgmental, descriptive feedback helps counter possible areas of reactivity and helps trainees stay in an open learning stance.

VIGNETTE

Julie is showing a video recording to her supervisor. The client is telling one story after another about her week: "And then actually Sunday was fun. We all went to a movie, and then we had breakfast for dinner at home. Eggs, pancakes, maple syrup, bacon—you know we all love that."

The client keeps going, and the therapist says nothing. Occasionally she nods or chimes in with reflective statements like, "It sounds like that was fun." She responds in the same way when the client describes an argument she had with her husband: "I was home with the kids making dinner, having worked all day, and he came home, dropped his bag, and said he had to go to the gym. He had to." The therapist says, "Oh, he had to."

We stop the recording. The supervisee says she knows she is just letting the client talk and tell stories, reporting and not relating. The supervisor suggests watching the vignette again to track the client and looking for entry points together. "She is telling stories in words, and her body is telling a story, too," says the supervisor. "Where on the triangle might we plot her? If we intuited her core feeling, what might it be?"

Supervisees often feel shame when they "let" clients talk. They know there is a correct way to work in AEDP, and this is not it! We have two acronyms to teach supervisees to pay attention to what they are doing: WAIT and WAIL:

- WAIT = Why am I talking?
- WAIL = Why am I listening?

We know that we are supposed to be trying to help clients drop down into their somatic experience—to the bottom of the triangle. That said, supervisees sometimes offer reasons for thinking that the talking is productive or the client needs to tell me all of this. Sometimes telling a particular story is important. If so, we have ways to keep the emotion focused and somatic awareness alive throughout the story. For instance, the supervisor might say, "I want to hear everything, and I wonder if we can keep the bandwidth wide, so we can track together how you are feeling and how your body is talking as you tell me this." Again, self-disclosure and normalizing are useful here; knowing that we, as AEDP therapists, often feel shame ourselves undos aloneness and helps the supervisor and supervisee connect in a nonhierarchical way. We often share Elizabeth Schoettle's (2009) research about the experiences of therapists practicing AEDP:

> One participant . . . bravely described the shame he feels when he has a hard time moving clients from defenses (State 1, top of the triangle) to core affect (aka core feeling, State 2 bottom of the triangle). He hypothesized that shame is common in AEDP clinicians

and speculated that it may be less common for clinicians working in theories where the client stays in defense, because clinicians would not have the same expectations of themselves. To know that colleagues also feel shame (or other negative feelings) could be relieving to AEDP clinicians and give them permission to be more forthcoming with their peers and supervisors. (p. 116)

CONCLUSION

When we adapt to our different supervisees' attachment styles and levels of experience, they can stop worrying about how they can avoid criticism and shame, and, instead, orient to how they can make the most of supervision. In the next chapter, we describe two different ways that we develop AEDP supervisors, and we discuss AEDP strategies for self-care.

6

Supervisor Development and Self-Care

We received little formal training as we expanded from clinicians to supervisors. We learned from our own supervisors and our own experiences in supervision, and from accelerated experiential dynamic psychotherapy (AEDP) and practice. This lack of formal training has been one of the factors that motivated us to develop clear learning paths in AEDP as we train and supervise therapists and as we develop training for supervisors.

As the AEDP Institute expands nationally and internationally, we are developing a supervisor training program. To become a certified AEDP supervisor, one must first become a certified AEDP therapist and then go through a supervisory training process. Therapists become certified AEDP supervisors by following two paths: (a) We train therapists to become supervisory "assistants" during experiential exercises; and (b) we have a formal group and individual training process for supervisors-in-training.

http://dx.doi.org/10.1037/0000016-007
Supervision Essentials for Accelerated Experiential Dynamic Psychotherapy, by N. C. N. Prenn and D. Fosha

SUPERVISORY ASSISTANTS

In Essential Skills courses at the AEDP Institute, we train therapists to act as supervisory assistants in group experiential exercises. We improve our teaching and training through collaboration with our assistants, who are working directly with three participants for 4½ hours of hands-on skills training each 3-day weekend. We get instant feedback on whether supervisory assistants are effective in teaching our learning objectives for each weekend.

The experiential exercises involve a therapist, client, and witness working together, and one assistant is assigned to each triad. The group is given a different prompt each day, such as: "Tell me about something that you have recently accomplished or something that you feel good about." Each course participant works for 25 minutes in each role: as the therapist practicing specific skills, the client receiving the skills, and the witness tracking their internal experience moment-to-moment as the exercise unfolds. Over each 3-day weekend, assistants lead participants in practicing five to 10 discrete skills, such as slowing down, affirming, moment-to-moment tracking, entry points, anxiety regulating, defense recognition, self-disclosing, metaprocessing, privileging the positive, transformance detection, and somatic focus. Through detailed evaluations from participants in our courses, we gain clear and almost immediate feedback of where our assistants need to improve their skills in training. The course leader then takes time with each assistant to go through the evaluations and process the feedback. In this way, we cocreate and formulate a plan for supervisory assistants to improve their live supervising. Areas that need work typically include slowing down and taking the time to set up the exercise; setting clear expectations about how the assistant will give feedback to course members; and addressing frame issues, such as keeping time, stopping personal work that is too evocative, being evenhanded with all members of the triad, giving enough feedback so that participants feel they are learning, and not giving too much feedback so that participants feel unsuccessful, shamed, or overloaded.

We have found that therapists develop quickly in their roles as supervisory assistants. Over a typical five-weekend Essential Skills course, most new assistants move through recognizable stages (McNeill & Stoltenberg, 2016, in this Clinical Supervision Essentials Series) of supervisor development: initial role-entry shock, crisis, or imposter feelings in the first weekend followed by a focus on themselves and personalization of successes or failures accompanied by heightened anxiety and enthusiasm and excitement. By the fourth or fifth weekend, the focus changes to confidence, a natural assumption of the assistant identity, role security, and an understanding and the experience of knowing what is normative and predictable in a triad. By this point, assistants recognize that a typical weekend goes a particular way: Fridays are group-forming, Saturdays are more settled, and Sundays are bittersweet as an intimate triad says goodbye.

It's important to acknowledge when things don't go well. A recent skills course participant shared how relieved she felt when Prenn asked, "Who did not feel successful in the exercise this afternoon?" Several participants shared where they felt stumped. "You are right," Prenn answered. "That is a hard skill to practice, and I can see that we need to make the steps to that skill clearer. I am pained that it was hard. Thank you for letting me know." This is a win–win scenario: The supervisee–trainee feels heard and the course leader has the information she needs to improve her teaching. Metaprocessing, as always, helps both supervisor and supervisee grow.

Tailoring live supervision to the needs of three different group members who are in a vulnerable position and are practicing skills they have not tried before requires strong group leadership and the setting of clear expectations to keep the triad work safe. There is quite a big difference between teaching in the here-and-now a group of three versus supervising an individual or ongoing group of supervisees in a supervisory hour, in the privacy of one's office, from recorded sessions.

SUPERVISORY TRAINING PROGRAM

The second pathway to becoming a certified AEDP supervisor is a yearlong supervisor training program during which aspiring supervisors supervise each other under the guidance of a senior faculty member. Each supervisee shows a videorecording of his or her work with a client and is supervised live by a group member (who, in turn, is supervised in his or her supervision by the senior faculty member). We videorecord the entire group experience. It is a powerful experience to be witnessed by one's peers and to have recordings of this learning to review. We have learned how essential the beginning and end of these sessions is and also how layered the work is. When Prenn is supervising the supervision, she needs to know what each supervisor wants to learn and practice, and how that interfaces with what the supervisee wants to learn and what the client's goals are, as well.

We consider questions such as parallel process, how much emotion processing to do in supervision, the teach/treat line, and how different the supervising experience can feel, depending on the client and the state he or she is in with the therapist. It is important to balance the flow of the recorded session with stopping for moment-to-moment tracking and teaching moments. The course culminates in each group member's writing a paper that reflects on their growth and learning as a supervisor and specifically expands on aspects of AEDP theory as it translates into AEDP supervision.

Mentoring

Mentoring supervisees is a big part of AEDP. It comes naturally from the attachment stance of AEDP. Mentoring takes many forms: affirming particular qualities, ideas, or insights of supervisees and encouraging them to share them on the AEDP Listserv (see Suggested Readings, this volume, for more information); encouraging supervisees to write up cases for *Transformance: The AEDP Journal* and elsewhere; and inviting them to do presentations of cases at AEDP workshops. Professionals who have been mentored experience greater career satisfaction when they perceive the mentoring as not fault-finding, exploitative, or controlling (DeCastro, Griffith, Ubel, Stewart, & Reshma, 2014). Supportive mentoring through every stage of the AEDP training is the norm.

Prenn benefited from being mentored by Diana Fosha, Ben Lipton, and Ron Frederick. This meant that as she began supervising individuals and groups and later began presenting at conferences and teaching the AEDP Essential Skills courses, she had concrete help and encouragement. Now, in turn, Prenn enjoys enormous professional satisfaction in mentoring others.

Supervisor Burnout

Harrison and Westwood (2009) set out to investigate what characterizes the practices of "master therapists" and what they do to prevent burnout.[1] A novel and unexpected finding of their research was that "many therapists described feeling invigorated rather than depleted by their intimate empathic engagement with clients" and that "the ability to establish a deep, intimate, therapeutic alliance based upon presence, heartfelt concern, and love is an important aspect of wellbeing and professional satisfaction for many of these clinicians" (p. 211). AEDP therapy and supervision privilege the positive, and the work often feels good—these are great protectors against vicarious traumatization and supervisor (and therapist) burnout. It is hard not to smile along with Michael Glavin (see Chapter 1) and say that AEDP supervision is different from other supervisions because it feels good!

Harrison and Westwood (2009) identified nine protective practices to prevent burnout. We discuss the four that are most salient: a community to counter isolation, mindful self-awareness, exquisite empathy, and active optimism.

Community

AEDP is an active community that encourages gathering in person and online. Our therapists jump at opportunities to attend ongoing training and volunteer for a variety of professional opportunities worldwide: moderating the Listserv; hosting a "salon" to gather local AEDP therapists; and assisting at workshops, immersion courses, and skills courses. Our Listserv is a remarkably active forum for AEDP therapists around

---

[1] See also the excellent self-care checklist compiled by Norcross and Guy (2007).

the world to undo aloneness by sharing a triumph or to despair with their colleagues online.

Supervisor and peer availability also are crucial. We often say, "Text me to let me know how it went and if you'd like to talk it over." Group members offer support outside of supervision groups: "You have my cell number. Call me if you'd like backup." We can face together what is overwhelming to endure alone.

Mindful Self-Awareness

"[P]resent-focused attending to minute, ongoing shifts in mind, body, and the surrounding world" (Harrison & Westwood, 2009, p. 4) corresponds to AEDP's moment-to-moment tracking, which we also describe in our teaching as *interpersonal mindfulness*. In many ways, moment-to-moment tracking in therapy and supervision *is* mindfulness practice. Mindfulness increases "patience, presence and compassion" (p. 4).

Exquisite Empathy

Empathy is the cornerstone of AEDP, even when our relationship is not on track or when anger and assertiveness are necessary parts of attunement. A focus on what is happening in the moment keeps the work lively, zestful, vital, and energizing for all involved. These are sure protections against compassion fatigue and burnout.

Active Optimism

Some optimists might passively hope for the best, but active optimism suggests that we can work toward the best outcome. We know that our clients can and do heal because we see it every day. We have hope and faith that when we walk together through pain and suffering, we feel the connection and pleasure that are its accompaniment.

Supervisors are vulnerable to dynamic experiences and over the lifespan confront as many life challenges and stressors as anyone else. We are grateful to be armed with the protective factors inherent to AEDP, including our responsive community and our shared excitement about this endeavor.

CONCLUSION

In this chapter, we highlighted how important specific supervisor training is and described two pathways that we have developed to train AEDP
therapists to learn the knowledge, capacities, and new skills they need to
become AEDP supervisors. We highlighted the importance of collaboration, feedback, and metaprocessing in AEDP supervisor training. We
ended with how the AEDP community, the practice of mindful awareness,
and active optimism keep AEDP supervision vitalizing and enlivening for
all involved.

7

Research Support for the AEDP Supervisory Approach

*At our core, we believe in the power of and potential
for supervision to be supremely transformative.*

(Watkins, 2012, p. 193)

In a series of important contributions (Watkins, 1997, 2012; Watkins, Budge, & Callahan, 2015; Watkins & Riggs, 2012), Edward Watkins called for rigor in our thinking about clinical supervision through research on what is effective. Along with others (e.g., Falender & Shafranske, 2017), Watkins articulated essential criteria for what constitutes high-quality psychotherapy supervision in the new millennium. In this chapter, we review those criteria and other common factors, and we describe how they apply to accelerated experiential dynamic psychotherapy (AEDP)

The authors wish to thank Shigeru Iwakabe from Ochanomizu University in Tokyo for invaluable help with this chapter.

http://dx.doi.org/10.1037/0000016-008

supervision. We also review research on AEDP (Iwakabe & Conceição, 2015; Lee, 2015; Piliero, 2004; Schoettle, 2009), AEDP training (Faerstein & Levenson, 2016; Iwakabe & Conceição, 2016), and AEDP supervision (Conceição, Iwakabe, Edlin, et al., 2016) itself to see how research can elucidate the mechanisms that make AEDP a transformative supervision.

ESSENTIAL QUALITIES OF EFFECTIVE SUPERVISION

To be effective, supervision must be competency-based (Falender & Shafranske, 2017), "particularized," "energized" (Watkins, 2012, pp. 193, 197), and evidence based (Milne, 2009; Milne, Aylott, Fitzpatrick, & Ellis, 2008). Clinical supervision in AEDP satisfies all four criteria.

AEDP's *competencies* are the skills described by the AEDP Fidelity Scale (AEDP-FS; see Chapter 4 and https://www.aedpinstitute.org/; see also Faerstein & Levenson, 2016). AEDP ably and effectively translates "therapist declarative knowledge into procedural knowledge" (Watkins, 2012, p. 196), and, paradoxically, AEDP supervision starts with procedural knowledge and then gradually weaves in declarative knowledge. Once procedural competence is attained, we build on that foundation of already demonstrated procedural knowledge through metaprocessing supervisees' experience of their own competence. We then broaden, augment, and enrich that procedural knowledge, now with a felt sense component—with the declarative knowledge of AEDP's healing oriented theory and formulations.

Next, AEDP supervision, like AEDP therapy, is, by its fundamental nature, individualized or particularized in a way that includes, but goes beyond, paying attention to supervisees' differences in learning styles and developmental levels. AEDP supervision focuses on moment-to-moment tracking, emergence, and direction-defining attention to moments of change for the better. Thus, each supervisee and each supervisory dyad in AEDP is seen and experienced as unique, emergent, self-defining, and self-organizing (Conceição, Iwakabe, Edlin, et al., 2016).

Similarly with energizing: As described in Chapter 3 and in the companion DVD (Fosha, 2016) to this book, supervision sessions often end with shared excitement, high spirits, inspiration, energy, and mastery affects.

AEDP's phenomenologically precise focus on the micro- and macroprocesses of change for the better, positive affects, positive somatic–affective markers that accompany and emerge from the transformational process, and transformational affects organically results in AEDP clinical supervision's being vital, energized, emergent, and regularly and systematically punctuated by "faith, hope, awe and wonder" (Watkins, 2012, p. 193) in the supervisor and supervisee. A recently completed qualitative study (Iwakabe & Conceição, 2016) of clinicians' experiences in AEDP generated three categories that best organized the data, one of which was vitality, energy, and flow. That category speaks to the centrality of these experiences in AEDP supervision.

To be effective, supervision needs to be evidence based. What constitutes *evidence* and how the term is construed are complex questions. As experts in the field of research on supervision (Ellis & Ladany, 1997; Watkins, 1997, 2012) have acknowledged, research on what makes supervision effective is still in its infancy. The American Psychological Association Clinical Supervision Essentials series (of which this book is a part) is making a significant contribution to our comparative knowledge base. More specifically, we are proud to have an empirical study that supports the effectiveness of AEDP training in increasing clinicians' base of knowledge and their sense of competence in AEDP (Faerstein & Levenson, 2016). However, AEDP's evidentiary basis goes beyond that. To adapt and paraphrase a line of argument articulated by Greg Johanson (2014) about Hakomi therapy, in AEDP, research findings are engaged critically in dialogue with the clinical experience and phenomenology of AEDP. This is precisely how AEDP evolved and continues to grow. AEDP is pioneering aspects of supervision, such as the use of metaprocessing, reliance on video recording, focus on healing, articulation of a transformational phenomenology, privileging of positive affects, and dyadic affect regulation. AEDP also is pioneering the use of a theory of change—rather than theories of pathology or deficiency—to inform the practice of supervision, and has been doing so from its inception—even before those ideas were in the Zeitgeist and endorsed by empirical studies.

Furthermore, AEDP uses findings from beyond psychotherapy and psychotherapy supervision to support, enhance, and develop its practices. For example, our work is informed by emergent developments in consilient fields, such as neuroplasticity (Doidge, 2007; Murty & Adcock, 2013; Shohamy & Adcock, 2010), affective neuroscience (e.g., Damasio, 2010; Panksepp, 1998; Panksepp & Biven, 2012), attachment and emotion theories (e.g., Bowlby, 1982, 1991; Darwin, 1872/1965; Ekman, Levenson, & Friesen, 1983; Fonagy & Target, 1998; Fredrickson, 2001, 2009; Keltner, 2009; Main, 1999), interpersonal neurobiology (Siegel, 2010), developmental studies (e.g., Beebe & Lachmann, 1994; Stern, 1985; Tronick, 1998), and transformational studies (e.g., W. R. Miller & C'de Baca, 2001; Stern et al., 1998).

Barbara Fredrickson (2001, 2009) produced paradigm-shifting work on the adaptive value of positive emotions and the broaden-and-build theory of positive affects. She and her colleagues conducted significant empirical research on resilience, upward spirals, and flourishing (Fredrickson & Losada, 2005; Tugade & Fredrickson, 2004), phenomena commonly encountered in AEDP and AEDP supervision and less commonly occurring, if at all, in other models of supervision. Fredrickson pointed out that positive emotions often lead to *cognitive broadening*, which is the expansion of thought-action repertoires. The broaden-and-build model provides a powerful explanation of how learning occurs in environments that privilege positive emotions and experiences. When focused on and encouraged, as they are in the AEDP practice of metaprocessing, positive emotions lead to the expansion of thought-action repertoires, which sets into motion an upward spiral of positive healing and growth, and the creation of new meaning and understanding (Fosha, 2009a, 2013c; Fredrickson, 2001; Tronick, 2009). Fredrickson's entire body of work provides a powerful theoretical and empirical foundation for key paradigmatic aspects of AEDP and AEDP supervision, and for the mechanisms that make AEDP supervision transformative.

ACCOUNTABILITY AND THE USE OF VIDEO IN AEDP SUPERVISION: ASSESSMENT, SELF-ASSESSMENT, AND IMMEDIATE FEEDBACK

Watkins (2012; Watkins & Milne, 2014) emphasized the importance of accountability in supervision and of assessment, self-assessment, and immediate feedback for effective learning. In AEDP, conducting supervision from video recordings of the supervisee's actual therapy sessions rather than self-report allows for accurate assessment and self-assessment. Video review allows for immediate feedback, access to actual supervisee and client verbal and nonverbal behaviors, and targeted and precise supervision interventions (Goodyear & Nelson, 1997). Efficacy outcome studies have shown that soliciting and responding appropriately to client feedback significantly contributes to an improved outcome for the client and to the development of the therapist (Anker, Duncan, & Sparks, 2009; Duncan, 2010; Duncan, Solovey, & Rusk, 1992). The video recording provides that de facto feedback to the therapist—feedback that is decoded, interpreted, and elaborated in the supervision session; there, the feedback is held and supported within the cocreated safety of AEDP supervision.

For the motivated supervisee, the act of preparing for supervision by reviewing a recording of a session, and the possibility of doing so repeatedly, looking for specific passages in a session constitute *deliberate practice*, defined by S. D. Miller, Hubble, and Duncan (2007) as working to reach specific objectives that are just a little beyond one's current level of skillfulness. Having a video recording to review after the fact before and after a supervision session allows for those so motivated to use deliberate practice.

COMMON FACTORS IN SUPERVISION

Despite the methodological criticisms of most empirical studies on clinical supervision, it is clear that the supervisory relationship is the most important variable in supervision (Angus & Kagan, 2007; Budge & Wampold, 2015; Ellis & Ladany, 1997; Watkins, 2012; Watkins & Milne, 2014; Watkins et al., 2015). Empathy, goal consensus, collaboration, and the working alliance are demonstrably effective, according to the criteria adopted from empirically supported treatments (Norcross & Wampold, 2011). Because the positive relationship between these variables and psychotherapy outcomes has been established, we extend them to psychotherapy supervision and hypothesize that these aspects—empathy, goal consensus, and collaboration—make AEDP supervision so powerful in a trainee's self-report. The use of the AEDP-FS as a supervisory tool only furthers the ability of supervisors and supervisees to be in alignment with goal consensus.

AEDP has a coherent, theory-driven understanding (Milne et al., 2008) of how relationships become change agents. This relational understanding informs specific supervisory interventions that are in accord with what is deemed to be high-quality supervision (Falender & Shafranske, 2004, 2017). Whether engaged in resolving conflict, giving feedback, repairing disruptions, or engaging in self-disclosure, AEDP supervisors seek to undo the supervisee's aloneness and contribute to dyadic affect regulation while working to increase the supervisee's clinical competence.

Along with a theory of change based on the therapeutic relationship, AEDP puts into practice other common factors found in successful supervision, including supervisory immediacy, self-disclosure in the supervisory relationship, and the addressing of conflicts between supervisor and supervisee. Research has shown that phenomena characterized by *therapeutic immediacy*, the in-session processing of the therapeutic relationship, make a powerful contribution to positive outcome in therapy (Hill, 2004; Mayotte-Blum et al., 2012). Hill (2009) and Hill and Knox (2009) concluded that the benefits of such therapeutic interactions are clear: Clients are provided with interpersonal feedback, and ruptures in the therapeutic relationship can be resolved or repaired, which helps clients make changes in their relationship patterns outside therapy. More recently, Hill's (2004) definition has been expanded to capture the dyadic aspects of the therapeutic relationship (Iwakabe & Conceição, 2016; Kuutmann & Hilsenroth, 2012; Mayotte-Blum et al., 2012). Thus expanded, therapeutic immediacy includes various phenomena: the client or therapist's expression of in-session emotional reactions to each other, the therapist's inquiry into the client's reaction to the therapy or the therapist, the therapist's disclosure of his or her own impressions of the client and therapy, the therapist's affirmation and validation of client's feelings, and the therapist's encouragement to explore parallels between the therapy relationship and external relationships with significant others (Mayotte-Blum et al., 2012). AEDP's metatherapeutic processing has been described as a particular class of therapeutic immediacy events "in which a piece of successful therapeutic work just completed is reviewed and processed by both therapist and client" (Iwakabe & Conceição, 2016, p. 5). These are all formal and explicit aspects of AEDP.

Supervisory Immediacy

Extrapolating from those lines of psychotherapy research, we extend the notion of therapeutic immediacy and its constituent elements into the realm of clinical supervision by introducing the construct of *supervisory immediacy*. This construct includes various phenomena that—as we have discussed in earlier chapters—are formal and explicit aspects of AEDP: supervisee-to-supervisor expression of in-session emotional reactions to each other or to the client being worked with, supervisory inquiry into the supervisee's reaction to the supervision or the supervisor, the therapist's disclosure of his or her own impressions of the client and therapy, the supervisor's affirmation and validation of the supervisee's clinical world, and the supervisor's encouragement to explore how the supervisee's experience of supervision and of the supervisor's interventions touches him or her.

Self-Disclosure as an Important Aspect of Supervisory Immediacy

The supervisor self-discloses and thus models and encourages the supervisee's disclosure, and builds trust and an emotional connection. Ladany and Walker (2003) suggested that supervisory disclosures directly influence the emotional-bond component of the supervisory alliance by communicating trust. Disclosures by the supervisor may model and encourage supervisee self-disclosure.

Ladany, Hill, Corbett, and Nutt (1996) and Yourman and Farber (1996) reported high rates of supervisees' not disclosing uncomfortable experiences to their supervisors. Although nothing is totally fail-safe, several specific aspects of AEDP supervision are noteworthy in this context. Modeling by the supervisor of his or her judicious self-disclosure helps create safety for the supervisee to do likewise. In addition, the focus on moment-to-moment tracking of experience makes the supervisee and supervisor more likely to be aware of the supervisee's discomfort, guardedness, and inauthenticity. When supervisors notice a supervisee who is distant, withdrawn, or trying to please, they invite them to internally explore whether anything is wrong, and then they invite them, if they wish to do so, to share their struggles or discomforts openly with the supervisors. When supervisees make such disclosures, the supervisors invariably affirm them for their courage and integrity.

Conflicts Between Supervisor and Supervisee Addressed Explicitly, Then Experientially Explored, Then Metaprocessed

Moskowitz and Rupert (1983) provided insight into what effective supervisors did to handle conflict, given that 38% of their sample reported having had a major conflict with a supervisor. Of the 158 participants, 86% stated a strong preference that the supervisor identify and initiate discussion of the conflict situation. How supervisors conduct our relationships in AEDP is informed by our deep understanding of attachment theory: It is the responsibility of the person perceived as older and wiser, in this case, the AEDP supervisor, to take the initiative to address any potential conflicts. As an attachment figure, in AEDP supervision, the supervisor follows and leads: follows when the process is flowing and leads when there are problems. Thus, we concur with the inclination of the 86% and agree that the supervisor should initiate the difficult conversation (see also Kaufman, 1996). When the attachment figure takes the lead, it decreases the shame of the more vulnerable partner.

Interestingly, in the same study (Moskowitz & Rupert, 1983), many trainees also reported that when they attempted to complain, discuss conflict, or provide negative feedback, the supervisor became confrontational, defensive, accusatory, or outright angry. It is critical for supervisors to respond nondefensively to supervisees' negative feedback. In AEDP, not only do supervisors seek to respond nondefensively, we ensure that we meet such supervisee actions with affirmation, validation, and appreciation: "How courageous of you to tell me that you haven't felt safe with me. I really appreciate your telling me so directly." By meeting such material with equanimity and understanding, not only can the conflicts in the supervisory relationship come out into the open, it is our goal that they do so in conditions of safety.

AEDP SUPERVISION AS A PATHWAY TO EXCELLENCE

S. D. Miller et al. (2007) became interested in investigating what differentiates the *supershrinks*, those therapists with client outcomes in the top 25%, from all other therapists on a normal distribution. Remarkably, their work didn't lead to identifying extraordinary individuals but to identifying extraordinary practices. Having discovered that supershrink behavior involves being "exquisitely attuned to the vicissitudes of client engagement" (S. D. Miller et al., 2007, p. 43), S. D. Miller et al. identified three additional key components of deliberate practice:

1. Determining one's own baseline of effectiveness: Supershrinks accurately self-assess what one does, and are mindful and accurate of what they capable of.
2. Getting feedback: Supershrinks depend on and are informed by the others, working in tandem to create a cycle of excellence.
3. Supershrinks engage in deliberate practice, "the amount of time specifically devoted to reaching for objectives just beyond one's level of proficiency." (S. D. Miller et al., 2007, p. 41)

We were highly encouraged to learn of this work because it lends strong support to the standard practices of AEDP clinical supervision and of the AEDP model in general. It suggests that what for us is standard practice has the potential to make our trainees into supershrinks. Being exquisitely attuned to the vicissitudes of client engagement, that is, what we call moment-to-moment tracking, characterizes and underlies AEDP therapy and supervision and is something that we explicitly teach. Also, AEDP supervision and training's reliance on the use of video further allows accurate attunement to become an achievable reality and not a merely wished for, but unreachable, competency. Meanwhile, the use of the AEDP-FS in supervision is a formal way of determining one's baseline.

Getting feedback is the key goal of moment-to-moment tracking and metaprocessing. Deliberate practice is part and parcel of standard AEDP supervision methodology. The very process of preparing for a supervision session involves having a video recording ready and reviewing it one or more times to choose segments for presentation in supervision. Then, in the supervision itself, the supervisor and supervisee watch that recording together again and have the option of reviewing it again afterward in light of the supervisory process.

TRANSFORMATIVE SUPERVISION

Research into AEDP as a treatment modality is just beginning, so much is to be done to investigate the process and outcome in AEDP therapy and supervision.

Effectiveness

To date, AEDP empirical studies have shown the effectiveness of AEDP in a modified self-help protocol based on Frederick's (2009) work to reduce symptoms of depression and anxiety (Johansson, Björklund, Hornborg, et al., 2013; Johansson, Frederick, & Andersson, 2013; Johansson, Hesser, Ljótsson, Frederick, & Andersson, 2012; Lilliengren, Johansson, Lindqvist, Mechler, & Andersson, 2016). AEDP also has been shown to effect characterological changes that last until long after therapy has been completed (Piliero, 2004). Clients prefer experiential therapies over other therapies: Asked to compare the effectiveness of treatments, nearly 66% said that their affect-focused, experiential therapy was significantly better than their previous therapies (Piliero, 2004). At the time of this writing (2016), a major outcome study is underway to assess the effectiveness of AEDP therapy (Iwakabe, Fosha, & Edlin, 2016). Outcome and process measures are included, and each session of therapy is being video recorded and analyzed by the research team.

Mechanisms of Change

In an exploration of the experiences of AEDP therapists who help clients process difficult emotional experiences, Schoettle (2009) discovered that therapists' subjective experiences matched and mirrored those of their clients, state by state. Her research documented the power of right-brain-to-right-brain communication and resonant processes in AEDP. Iwakabe and Conceição (2015) conducted a methodologically rigorous task analytic study that identified component processes in clients' and therapists' metaprocessing experiences. Lee (2015) analyzed a different set of gold sample metatherapeutic processing examples and replicated Iwakabe and Conceição's work; both studies identified enlivenment as an important aspect of the client's affective experience during metaprocessing.

We currently have these three completed empirical studies on AEDP training and supervision, and more are in the works.

Effectiveness of AEDP Training

Faerstein and Levenson (2016) conducted a study to investigate the psychometric properties of a self-report measure of therapist fidelity to AEDP and to use this measure to evaluate the effectiveness of AEDP training, in this case the AEDP Immersion course. Using a three-step process, Levenson, Fosha, and therapists trained in AEDP developed the AEDP-FS (available at https://www.aedpinstitute.org/wp-content/uploads/2014/01/AEDP-Fidelity-Scale-Self-Report.pdf). First, Levenson, Fosha, and a group of AEDP Institute faculty listed those therapist behaviors considered to be important in practicing AEDP. After some refinements, Fosha asked therapists (via a Listserv) who had previously attended an AEDP Immersion course to describe "what makes AEDP AEDP." Levenson, Fosha, and AEDP faculty then selected the most essential items from the items generated. Those 22 items describe specific AEDP interventions and more general therapist behaviors. Each item is self-rated separately for knowledge and competence.

Approximately 250 therapists who participated in one of four 5-day Immersion courses on both the East and West Coasts of the United States filled out the AEDP-FS pre- and posttraining. In addition, 13 AEDP faculty completed the scale. Results were powerful. Significant increases in knowledge of AEDP principles and practices, and a sense of competence in putting those into practice, were found following exposure to the Immersion course. In addition, AEDP faculty reported significantly higher AEDP-FS scores than participants, and participants with more AEDP experience reported significantly higher pretest scores than participants with less AEDP experience. Furthermore, when the items on the AEDP-FS were analyzed, three strong factors emerged that were resonant with AEDP theory and fundamental understanding. In order of magnitude and importance, they were: the transformational factor; the experiential and/or somatic factor; and the AEDP therapeutic stance, with its emphasis on affirmation, delight, and cocreating secure attachment. The findings support our use of the AEDP-FS as a tool for describing essential AEDP interventions and for training AEDP therapists.

A Qualitative Study on Therapists' Experiences While Training in AEDP

Iwakabe and Conceição (2016) examined therapists' motivation for approaching AEDP training and their training, development, and change processes. They conducted in-depth, semistructured interviews with 18 therapists having varying levels of clinical experience and who received different amounts of exposure to AEDP training. Regarding one general question in the study—how the therapist is affected by working with an AEDP informed stance—one main cluster emerged from the grounded theory analyses, transformations in self, that pertained to changes of an experiential nature directly involving the experiencing self of the therapist. These comprised three categories: presence; willingness for shared connection; and vitality, energy, and flow.

One interesting result of that study highlighted that the shift from novice to experienced professional, which often is thought to require 10 to 15 years of experience—as described in Rønnestad and Skovholt's (2003) six-phase model of professional development—can be fostered much earlier in one's career. Characteristics usually attributed to this later phase (e.g., developing a personal clinical style congruent with one's personality, worldview, and interpersonal style; trusting the client; valuing the therapeutic relationship as a change agent; achieving a higher level of emotional involvement and openness; enhancing career satisfaction) emerged from the grounded theory analysis of those 18 interviews. According to Iwakabe and Conceição, AEDP seems to be explicitly training these capacities in trainees and supervisees from the get-go, irrespective of the trainees' age or experience. In particular, the therapists who participated in the study valued repetitive experiential exposure with numerous role rehearsals and video tracking, safe group dynamics permitting vulnerability and the soothing of self-wounds, processing painful moments of failing as pleasant moments of mastery, and acceptance and affirmation of the learner's self. Regarding supervision, participants mentioned AEDP's experiential and affirmative stance, and the use of video to anchor specific and concrete material.

A Qualitative Empirical Study of Change Processes in AEDP Supervision

To bring qualitative process research to supervision, Conceição, Iwakabe, Edlin, et al. (2016) presented a longitudinal case study of supervision in AEDP that captures the change processes fostered by that supervision process itself. Audio recordings of 24 supervision consultations done by the same supervisee–supervisor dyad (three sessions for each of eight clients) were transcribed and analyzed following the grounded theory method. One predominant category that emerged, voicing the therapist, appeared to serve experiential and relational purposes, both of which are core features of the AEDP model itself. Other categories emerged that are indicative of AEDP: affirmation, enthusiasm, delight and validation, removing pressure and negotiating, facilitating experiencing, metaprocessing, and sharing pleasant feelings and vulnerability.

CONCLUSION

Research into supervision processes is in its early days, and research into supervision processes in AEDP is in its infancy. Yet, there is a strong indication that AEDP supervision is on the right track, given its relational, experiential, and transformational supervisory interventions, which are thought to be necessary for supervision to be not only effective but also transformative.

As we end this book, we invite you to slow down for a minute and reflect on all we have experienced together over these seven chapters. Having intended the book more as a primer than a novel, we encourage you to read and reread the sections you found most helpful so that you can absorb the skills, knowledge, and capacities of a transformative supervision and get the structure of the magic of AEDP into your bones—or rather, we should say—into your procedural memory!

Suggested Readings

If this book has piqued your interest in accelerated experiential dynamic psychotherapy (AEDP), you can go to the AEDP Institute's website (https://www.aedpinstitute.org/) for books, free and downloadable articles and book chapters, and information about DVDs and upcoming training. Go to https://www.aedpinstitute.org/become-a-member/ to become a member of the AEDP Institute, which gives you access to the AEDP Listserv—a forum for lively clinical and theoretical discussions and referrals—and a subscription to *Transformance: The AEDP Journal*, a transcript-based journal. We also recommend the following books and articles:

Fosha, D. (2000). *The transforming power of affect: A model of accelerated change.* New York, NY: Basic Books.

This is a good place to begin reading about AEDP psychotherapy.

Fosha, D., Siegel, D. J., & Solomon, M. F. (Eds.). (2009). *The healing power of emotion: Affective neuroscience, development, & clinical practice.* New York, NY: Norton.

This book expands on the healing power of emotion and includes readings on affective neuroscience.

Frederick, R. (2009). *Living like you mean it: Use the wisdom and power of your emotions to get the life you really want.* San Francisco, CA: Jossey-Bass.

This book is easy to grasp and apply to yourself, and to give to clients.

Prenn, N. (2011). Mind the gap: AEDP interventions translating attachment theory into clinical practice. *Journal of Psychotherapy Integration, 21,* 308–329. http://dx.doi.org/10.1037/a0025491

This is a good, short read and is helpful if you are looking for ways to put AEDP into practice in your individual psychotherapy sessions.

Prenn, N. (2009). I second that emotion! On self-disclosure and its metaprocessing. In A. Bloomgarden & R. B. Menutti (Eds.), *Psychotherapist revealed: Therapists speak about self-disclosure in psychotherapy* (pp. 85–99). New York, NY: Routledge.

This is a compelling, fast read about self-disclosure and how Natasha Prenn came to her understanding of the importance of self-disclosure.

Russell, E. M. (2015). *Restoring resilience: Discovering your clients' capacity for healing.* New York, NY: Norton.

In this book, Eileen Russell greatly expands AEDP theory and the practice of positive affects and their role in healing and resilience.

References

Alpert, M. C. (1992). Accelerated empathic therapy: A new short-term dynamic psychotherapy. *International Journal of Short-Term Psychotherapy, 7,* 133–156.

American Psychological Association. (2010). *Ethical principles of psychologists and code of conduct (2002, Amended June 1, 2010).* Retrieved from http://www.apa.org/ethics/code/index.aspx

Angus, L., & Kagan, F. (2007). Empathic relational bonds and personal agency in psychotherapy: Implications for psychotherapy supervision, practice, and research. *Psychotherapy: Theory, Research, Practice, Training, 44,* 371–377. http://dx.doi.org/10.1037/0033-3204.44.4.371

Anker, M. G., Duncan, B. L., & Sparks, J. A. (2009). Using client feedback to improve couple therapy outcomes: A randomized clinical trial in a naturalistic setting. *Journal of Consulting and Clinical Psychology, 77,* 693–704. http://dx.doi.org/10.1037/a0016062

Badenoch, B. (2008). *Being a brain-wise therapist: A practical guide to interpersonal neurobiology.* New York, NY: Norton.

Beebe, B., & Lachmann, F. M. (1988). The contribution of mother–infant mutual influence to the origins of self and object representations. *Psychoanalytic Psychology, 5,* 305–337.

Beebe, B., & Lachmann, F. M. (1994). Representation and internalization in infancy: Three principles of salience. *Psychoanalytic Psychology, 11,* 127–165. http://dx.doi.org/10.1037/h0079530

Binder, J. L. (1993). Is it time to improve psychotherapy training? *Clinical Psychology Review, 13,* 301–318. http://dx.doi.org/10.1016/0272-7358(93)90015-E

Bollas, C. (1987). *The shadow of the object: Psychoanalysis of the unthought known.* New York, NY: Columbia University Press.

Bowlby, J. (1982). *Attachment and loss: Vol. 1. Attachment* (2nd ed.). New York, NY: Basic Books.

Bowlby, J. (1988). *A secure base: Parent–child attachment and healthy human development.* New York, NY: Basic Books.

Bowlby, J. (1991). Postscript. In C. M. Parkes, J. Stevenson-Hinde, & P. Marris (Eds.), *Attachment across the life cycle* (pp. 293–297). London, England: Routledge.

Bromberg, P. M. (1998). *Standing in the spaces: Essays on clinical process, trauma, and dissociation.* Mahwah, NJ: Analytic Press.

Bromberg, P. M. (2006). *Awakening the dreamer: Clinical journeys.* Mahwah, NJ: Analytic Press.

Bromberg, P. M. (2011). *The shadow of the tsunami and the growth of the relational mind.* New York, NY: Routledge.

Budge, S. L., & Wampold, B. E. (2015). The relationship: How it works. In O. C. G. Gelo, A. Pritz, & B. Rieken (Eds.), *Psychotherapy research: Foundations, process, and outcomes* (pp. 213–228). Dordrecht, The Netherlands: Springer.

Carifio, M. S., & Hess, A. K. (1987). Who is the ideal supervisor? *Professional Psychology: Research and Practice, 18,* 244–250. http://dx.doi.org/10.1037/0735-7028.18.3.244

Carter, C. S. (1998). Neuroendocrine perspectives on social attachment and love. *Psychoneuroendocrinology, 23,* 779–818. http://dx.doi.org/10.1016/S0306-4530(98)00055-9

Carter, C. S., & Porges, S. W. (2012). The biochemistry of love: An oxytocin hypothesis. *European Molecular Biology Organization Reports, 14,* 12–16. http://dx.doi.org/10.1038/embor.2012.191

Clausen, W. V. (Ed.). (1992). *Quis cutodiet ipsos custodies?* [Who will guard the guards?] (rev. ed.). London, England: Oxford University Press.

Conceição, N., Iwakabe, S., Edlin, J., Vaz-Velho, C., Rodrigues, C., & Gleiser, K. (2016, June 7). Supervising an integrative therapist into yet another approach: A case study on change processes of supervision facilitating assimilative integration [Webinar]. Presented at AEDP Faculty Hour Online.

Conceição, N., Rodrigues, C., Silva, A. I., Luz, C., Iwakabe, S., & Gleiser, K. (2016, June). *Supervising an integrative therapist into a specific approach: A case study on supervision of AEDP principles.* Paper presented at the 32nd International Conference of the Society for the Exploration of Psychotherapy Integration, Dublin, Ireland.

Damasio, A. R. (2010). *Self comes to mind: Constructing the conscious brain.* New York, NY: Pantheon Books.

Darwin, C. (1965). *The expression of emotion in man and animals.* Chicago, IL: University of Chicago Press. (Original work published 1872)

Davanloo, H. (1990). *Unlocking the unconscious: Selected papers of Habib Davanloo.* New York, NY: Wiley.

Davanloo, H. (1995). Intensive short-term dynamic psychotherapy: Spectrum of psychoneurotic disorders. *International Journal of Short-Term Psychotherapy, 10,* 121–155.

Davanloo, H. (2000). *Intensive short-term dynamic psychotherapy: Selected papers of Habib Davanloo, MD.* Chichester, England: Wiley.

DeCastro, R., Griffith, K. A., Ubel, P. A., Stewart, A., & Reshma, J. (2014). Mentoring and the career satisfaction of male and female academic medical faculty. *Academic Medicine, 89,* 301–311.

Della Selva, P. C. (1996). *Intensive short-term dynamic psychotherapy.* New York, NY: Wiley.

Doidge, N. (2007). *The brain that changes itself: Stories of personal triumph from the frontiers of brain science.* New York, NY: Penguin Books.

Duncan, B. L. (2010). *On becoming a better therapist.* Washington, DC: American Psychological Association. http://dx.doi.org/10.1037/12080-000

Duncan, B. L., Solovey, A. D., & Rusk, G. S. (1992). *Changing the rules: A client-directed approach to therapy.* New York, NY: Guilford Press.

Ecker, B., Ticic, R., & Hulley, L. (2012). *Unlocking the emotional brain: Eliminating symptoms at their roots using memory reconsolidation.* New York, NY: Routledge.

Ekman, P. (1984). Expression and the nature of emotion. In K. R. Scherer & P. Ekman (Eds.), *Approaches to emotion* (pp. 319–343). Hillsdale, NJ: Erlbaum.

Ekman, P., Levenson, R. W., & Friesen, W. V. (1983). Autonomic nervous system activity distinguishes among emotions. *Science, 221,* 1208–1210. http://dx.doi.org/10.1126/science.6612338

Ellis, M. V., & Ladany, N. (1997). Inferences concerning supervisees and clients in clinical supervision: An integrative review. In C. E. Watkins, Jr. (Ed.), *Handbook of psychotherapy supervision* (pp. 447–507). Hoboken, NJ: Wiley.

Emde, R. N. (1981). Changing models of infancy and the nature of early development: Remodeling the foundation. *Journal of the American Psychoanalytic Association, 29,* 179–218. http://dx.doi.org/10.1177/000306518102900110

Emde, R. N. (1983). The prerepresentational self and its affective core. *Psychoanalytic Study of the Child, 38,* 165–192.

Emde, R. N. (1988). Development terminable and interminable. I. Innate and motivational factors from infancy. *International Journal of Psychoanalysis, 69,* 23–42.

Ezriel, H. (1952). Notes on psychoanalytic group therapy. II. Interpretation and research. *Psychiatry: Journal for the Study of Interpersonal Processes, 15,* 119–126.

Faerstein, I., & Levenson, H. (2016). Validation of a fidelity scale for accelerated-experiential dynamic psychotherapy. *Journal of Psychotherapy Integration, 26,* 172–185. http://dx.doi.org/10.1037/int0000020

Falender, C. A., & Shafranske, E. P. (2004). *Clinical supervision: A competency-based approach.* Washington, DC: American Psychological Association. http://dx.doi.org/10.1037/10806-000

Falender, C. A., & Shafranske, E. P. (2017). *Supervision essentials for the practice of competency-based supervision.* Washington, DC: American Psychological Association.

Farber, B. A. (2006). *Self-disclosure in psychotherapy.* New York, NY: Guilford Press.

Ferenczi, S. L. (1933). Confusion of tongues between adults and the child (E. Mosbacher, Trans.). In M. Balint (Ed.), *Further contributions to the problems and methods of psychoanalysis* (pp. 156–167). New York, NY: Brunner/Mazel.

Fonagy, P., Steele, M., Steele, H., Moran, G., & Higgitt, A. (1991). The capacity for understanding mental states: The reflective self in parent and child and its significance for secure attachment. *Infant Mental Health Journal, 12,* 201–218. http://dx.doi.org/10.1002/1097-0355(199123)12:3<201::AID-IMHJ2280120307>3.0.CO;2-7

Fonagy, P., & Target, M. (1998). Mentalization and the changing aims of child psychoanalysis. *Psychoanalytic Dialogues, 8,* 87–114. http://dx.doi.org/10.1080/10481889809539235

Fosha, D. (2000a). Meta-therapeutic processes and the affects of transformation: Affirmation and the healing affects. *Journal of Psychotherapy Integration, 10,* 71–97. http://dx.doi.org/10.1023/A:1009422511959

Fosha, D. (2000b). *The transforming power of affect: A model of accelerated change.* New York, NY: Basic Books.

Fosha, D. (2001). The dyadic regulation of affect. *Journal of Clinical Psychology/In Session, 57,* 227–242.

Fosha, D. (2002). The activation of affective change processes in accelerated experiential-dynamic psychotherapy (AEDP). In F. W. Kaslow & J. J. Magnavita (Eds.), *Comprehensive handbook of psychotherapy: Vol. 1. Psychodynamic/object relations* (pp. 309–343). Hoboken, NJ: Wiley.

Fosha, D. (2004). 'Nothing that feels bad is ever the last step': The role of positive emotions in experiential work with difficult emotional experiences. *Clinical Psychology and Psychotherapy, 11,* 30–43.

Fosha, D. (2005). Emotion, true self, true other, core state: Toward a clinical theory of affective change process. *Psychoanalytic Review, 92,* 513–551. http://dx.doi.org/10.1521/prev.2005.92.4.513

Fosha, D. (2006). Quantum transformation in trauma and treatment: Traversing the crisis of healing change. *Journal of Clinical Psychology, 62,* 569–583.

Fosha, D. (2007). Transformance, recognition of self by self, and effective action. In K. J. Schneider (Ed.), *Existential–integrative psychotherapy: Guideposts to the core of practice* (pp. 290–320). New York, NY: Routledge.

Fosha, D. (2008). Recognition, vitality, passion. And love. *Constructivism in the Human Sciences, 12,* 57–77.

Fosha, D. (2009a). Emotion and recognition at work: Energy, vitality, pleasure, truth, desire & the emergent phenomenology of transformational experience. In D. Fosha, D. J. Siegel, & M. F. Solomon (Eds.), *The healing power of emotion: Affective neuroscience, development, clinical practice* (pp. 172–203). New York, NY: Norton.

Fosha, D. (2009b). Healing attachment trauma with attachment (. . . and then some!). In M. Kerman (Ed.), *Clinical pearls of wisdom: 21 leading therapists offer their key insights* (pp. 43–56). New York, NY: Norton.

Fosha, D. (2009c). Positive affects and the transformation of suffering into flourishing. In W. C. Bushell, E. L. Olivo, & N. D. Theise (Eds.), *Longevity, regeneration, and optimal health: Integrating Eastern and Western perspectives* (pp. 252–262). New York, NY: Wiley-Blackwell.

Fosha, D. (2013a). A heaven in a wild flower: Self, dissociation, and treatment in the context of the neurobiological core self. *Psychoanalytic Inquiry, 33,* 496–523. http://dx.doi.org/10.1080/07351690.2013.815067

Fosha, D. (2013b). Speculations on emergence: Working the edge of transformational experience and neuroplasticity. *International Neuropsychotherapy Magazine, 1,* 120–121.

Fosha, D. (2013c). Turbocharging the affects of healing and redressing the evolutionary tilt. In D. J. Siegel & Marion F. Solomon (Eds.), *Healing moments in psychotherapy* (pp. 129–168). New York, NY: Norton.

Fosha, D. (2016). *Accelerated experiential dynamic psychotherapy (AEDP) supervision* [DVD]. Washington, DC: American Psychological Association. Available from https://www.apa.org/pubs/videos/4310958.aspx

Fosha, D., & Slowiaczek, M. L. (1997). Techniques to accelerate dynamic psychotherapy. *American Journal of Psychotherapy, 51,* 229–251.

Fosha, D., & Yeung, D. (2006). AEDP exemplifies the seamless integration of emotional transformation and dyadic relatedness at work. In G. Stricker & J. Gold (Eds.), *A casebook of integrative psychotherapy* (pp. 165–184). Washington, DC: American Psychological Association. http://dx.doi.org/10.1037/11436-013

Frederick, R. (2005, November 5). AEDP core training course. Presented at the AEDP Institute, San Francisco, CA.

Frederick, R. (2009). *Living like you mean it: Use the wisdom and power of your emotions to get the life you really want.* San Francisco, CA: Jossey-Bass.

Fredrickson, B. L. (2001). The role of positive emotions in positive psychology: The broaden-and-build theory of positive emotions. *American Psychologist, 56*, 218–226. http://dx.doi.org/10.1037/0003-066X.56.3.218

Fredrickson, B. L. (2009). *Positivity: Groundbreaking research reveals how to embrace the hidden strength of positive emotions, overcome negativity, and thrive.* New York, NY: Random House.

Fredrickson, B. L., & Losada, M. F. (2005). Positive affect and the complex dynamics of human flourishing. *American Psychologist, 60*, 678–686. http://dx.doi.org/10.1037/0003-066X.60.7.678

Gendlin, E. T. (1981). *Focusing* (2nd ed.). New York, NY: Bantam Books.

Gendlin, E. T. (1996). *Focusing-oriented psychotherapy: A manual of the experiential method.* New York, NY: Guilford Press.

Goodyear, R. K., & Nelson, M. L. (1997). The major formats of psychotherapy supervision. In C. E. Watkins, Jr. (Ed.), *Handbook of psychotherapy supervision* (pp. 328–344). New York, NY: Wiley.

Greenberg, L. S., & Watson, J. C. (2005). *Emotion-focused therapy for depression.* Washington, DC: American Psychological Association.

Hanakawa, Y. (2011). Receiving loving gratitude: How a therapist's mindful embrace of a patient's gratitude facilitates transformance. *Transformance: The AEDP Journal, 2*, 1–19.

Harrison, R. L., & Westwood, M. J. (2009). Preventing vicarious traumatization of mental health therapists: Identifying protective practices. *Psychotherapy: Theory, Research, Practice, Training, 46*, 203–219. http://dx.doi.org/10.1037/a0016081

Hatfield, E., Cacioppo, J., & Rapson, R. L. (1992). Primitive emotional contagion. In M. S. Clark (Ed.), *Emotion and social behavior: Review of personality and social psychology* (Vol. 14, pp. 151–177). Newbury Park, CA: Sage.

Hendel, H. J. (in press). *The change triangle.* New York, NY: Random House.

Hill, C. E. (2004). *Helping skills: Facilitating exploration, insight, and action* (2nd ed.). Washington, DC: American Psychological Association.

Hill, C. E. (2009). *Helping skills: Facilitating exploration, insight, and action* (3rd ed.). Washington, DC: American Psychological Association.

Hill, C. E., & Knox, S. (2009). Processing the therapeutic relationship. *Psychotherapy Research, 19*, 13–29. http://dx.doi.org/10.1080/10503300802621206

Hughes, D. (2007). *Attachment-focused family therapy.* New York, NY: Norton.

Iwakabe, S., & Conceição, N. (2015). Metatherapeutic processing as a change-based therapeutic immediacy task: Building an initial process model using a task-analytic research strategy. *Journal of Psychotherapy Integration.* Advance online publication. Retrieved from http://psycnet.apa.org/doi/10.1037/int0000016

Iwakabe, S., & Conceição, N. (2016, June 7). A qualitative study on therapists working at the edge of experience: Therapists' change processes in AEDP training and practice [Webinar]. Presented at AEDP Faculty Hour Online.

Iwakabe, S., Fosha, D., & Edlin, J. (2016, May 23). Proposal for a 16-session AEDP outcome study [Webinar]. Presented at AEDP Faculty Hour Online.

James, W. (1985). *The varieties of religious experience: A study in human nature.* Cambridge, MA: Harvard University Press. (Original work published 1902)

Johanson, G. J. (2014). Somatic psychotherapy and the ambiguous face of research. *International Body Psychotherapy Journal, 13*, 61–85.

Johansson, R., Björklund, M., Hornborg, C., Karlsson, S., Hesser, H., Ljótsson, B., . . . Andersson, G. (2013). Affect-focused psychodynamic treatment for depression and anxiety through the Internet: A randomized controlled trial. *Peer Journal, 1:e102.* http://dx.doi.org/10.7717/peerj.102

Johansson, R., Frederick, R. J., & Andersson, G. (2013). Using the internet to provide psychodynamic psychotherapy. *Psychodynamic Psychiatry, 41*, 513–540. http://dx.doi.org/10.1521/pdps.2013.41.4.513

Johansson, R., Hesser, H., Ljótsson, B., Frederick, R. J., & Andersson, G. (2012). Transdiagnostic, affect-focused, psychodynamic, guided self-help for depression and anxiety through the Internet: Study protocol for a randomised controlled trial. *BMJ Open, 2,* e002167. http://dx.doi.org/10.1136/bmjopen-2012-002167.

Jourard, S. M. (1971). *Self-disclosure: An experimental analysis of the transparent self.* New York, NY: Wiley-Interscience.

Kaufman, G. (1996). *The psychology of shame: Theory and treatment of shame-based syndromes.* New York, NY: Springer.

Keltner, D. (2009). *Born to be good: The science of a meaningful life.* New York, NY: Norton.

Kuutmann, K., & Hilsenroth, M. J. (2012). Exploring in-session focus on the patient–therapist relationship: Patient characteristics, process, and outcome. *Clinical Psychology & Psychotherapy, 19*, 187–202. http://dx.doi.org/10.1002/cpp.743

Ladany, N., Hill, C. E., Corbett, M. M., & Nutt, E. A. (1996). Nature, extent, and importance of what psychotherapy trainees do not disclose to their supervisors. *Journal of Counseling Psychology, 43*, 10–24. http://dx.doi.org/10.1037/0022-0167.43.1.10

Ladany, N., Inman, A. G., Hill, C. E., Knox, S., Crook-Lyon, R. E., Thompson, B. J., . . . Walker, J. A. (2012). Corrective relational experiences in supervision. In L. G. Castonguay & C. E. Hill (Eds.), *Transformation in psychotherapy: Corrective experiences across cognitive behavioral, humanistic, and psychodynamic approaches* (pp. 335–352). Washington, DC: American Psychological Association.

Ladany, N., & Walker, J. A. (2003). Supervisor self-disclosure: Balancing the uncontrollable narcissist with the indomitable altruist. *Journal of Clinical Psychology, 59*, 611–621. http://dx.doi.org/10.1002/jclp.10164

Lamagna, J. (2016). Making good use of suffering: Intra-relational work with pathogenic affects. *Transformance: The AEDP Journal, 6*, 1–15.

Lee, A. (2015). *Building a model for metaprocessing: Exploration of a key change event in accelerated experiential dynamic psychotherapy (AEDP)* (Unpublished doctoral dissertation). Wright Institute, Berkeley, CA.

Levenson, H. (1995). *Time-limited dynamic psychotherapy.* New York, NY: Basic Books.

Lilliengren, P., Johansson, R., Lindqvist, K., Mechler, J., & Andersson, G. (2016). Efficacy of experiential dynamic therapy for psychiatric conditions: A meta-analysis of randomized controlled trials. *Psychotherapy, 51*, 90–104.

Lipton, B. (2013, May 8). *Walking the talk of attachment in AEDP.* Presentation at the AEDP Institute, New York, NY.

Lipton, B., & Fosha, D. (2011). Attachment as a transformative process in AEDP: Operationalizing the intersection of attachment theory and affective neuroscience. *Journal of Psychotherapy Integration, 21*, 253–279. http://dx.doi.org/10.1037/a0025421

Lyons-Ruth, K. (2006). The interface between attachment and intersubjectivity: Perspective from the longitudinal study of disorganized attachment. *Psychoanalytic Inquiry, 26*, 595–616. http://dx.doi.org/10.1080/07351690701310656

Main, M. (1995). Recent studies in attachment: Overview with selected implications for clinical work. In S. Goldberg, R. Muir, & J. Kerr (Eds.), *Attachment theory: Social, developmental and clinical perspectives* (pp. 407–472). Hillsdale, NJ: Analytic Press.

Main, M. (1999). Attachment theory: Eighteen points with suggestions for further studies [Epilogue]. In J. Cassidy & P. R. (Eds.), *Handbook of attachment: Theory, research and clinical applications* (pp. 845–888). New York, NY: Guilford Press.

Malan, D. (1999). *Individual psychotherapy and the science of psychodynamics* (2nd ed.). Oxford, England: Butterworth-Heinemann.

Maroda, K. J. (1998). *Seduction, surrender, and transformation. Emotional engagement in the analytic process.* Hillsdale, NJ: Analytic Press.

Maroda, K. J. (2004). *The power of countertransference: Innovations in analytic technique* (2nd ed., rev. & enl.). Hillsdale, NJ: Analytic Press.

Maroda, K. J. (2009). Less is more: An argument for the judicious use of self-disclosure. In A. Bloomgarden & R. B. Mennuti (Eds.), *Psychotherapist revealed: Psychotherapists speak about self-disclosure in psychotherapy* (pp. 17–29). New York, NY: Routledge.

Mayotte-Blum, J., Slavin-Mulford, J., Lehmann, M., Pesale, F., Becker-Matero, N., & Hilsenroth, M. (2012). Therapeutic immediacy across long-term psychodynamic psychotherapy: An evidence-based case study. *Journal of Counseling Psychology, 59*, 27–40. http://dx.doi.org/10.1037/a0026087

McCullough, L. (1997). *Changing character: Short-term anxiety-regulating psychotherapy for restructuring defenses, affects, and attachment.* New York, NY: Basic Books.

McCullough, L., Kuhn, N., Andrews, S., Kaplan, A., Wolf, J., & Hurley, C. L. (2003). *Treating affect phobia: A manual for short-term dynamic psychotherapy.* New York, NY: Guilford Press.

McNeill, B. W., & Stoltenberg, C. D. (2016). *Supervision essentials for the integrative developmental model.* Washington, DC: American Psychological Association.

Miller, S. D., Hubble, M. A., & Duncan, B. L. (2007). Supershrinks: Learning from the field's most effective practitioners. *Psychotherapy Networker, 31*, 36–45, 57.

Miller, W. R., & C'de Baca, J. C. (2001). *Quantum change: When epiphanies and sudden insights transform ordinary lives.* New York, NY: Guilford Press.

Milne, D. (2009). *Evidence-based clinical supervision: Principles and practice.* New York, NY: Wiley.

Milne, D., Aylott, H., Fitzpatrick, H., & Ellis, M. V. (2008). How does clinical supervision work? Using a "best evidence synthesis" approach to construct a basic model of supervision. *Clinical Supervisor, 27*, 170–190. http://dx.doi.org/10.1080/07325220802487915

Moskowitz, S. A., & Rupert, P. A. (1983). Conflict resolution within the supervisory relationship. *Professional Psychology: Research and Practice, 14*, 632–641. http://dx.doi.org/10.1037/0735-7028.14.5.632

Murty, V. P., & Adcock, R. A. (2013). Enriched encoding: Reward motivation organizes cortical networks to enhance hippocampal encoding of unexpected events. *Cerebral Cortex, 24*, 2160–2168.

Norcross, J. C., & Guy, J. D., Jr. (2007). *Leaving it at the office: A guide to psychotherapist care.* New York, NY: Guilford Press.

Norcross, J. C., & Wampold, B. E. (2011). Evidence-based therapy relationships: Research conclusions and clinical practices. *Psychotherapy, 48*, 98–102. http://dx.doi.org/10.1037/a0022161

Pally, R. (2000). *The mind–brain relationship.* London, England: Karnac Books.

Panksepp, J. (1998). *Affective neuroscience: The foundations of human and animal emotions.* New York, NY: Oxford University Press.

Panksepp, J., & Biven, L. (2012). *The archaeology of mind: Origins of human emotions.* New York, NY: Norton.

Panksepp, J., & Northoff, G. (2009). The trans-species core SELF: The emergence of active cultural and neuro-ecological agents through self-related processing within subcortical–cortical midline networks. *Consciousness and Cognition, 18,* 193–215.

Pearson, J. L., Cohn, D. A., Cowan, P. A., & Cowan, C. P. (1994). Earned- and continuous-security in adult attachment: Relation to depressive symptomatology and parenting style. *Development and Psychopathology, 6,* 359–373. http://dx.doi.org/10.1017/S0954579400004636

Piliero, S. (2004). *Clients reflect upon their affect-focused, experiential psychotherapy: A retrospective study* (Unpublished doctoral dissertation). Adelphi University, Garden City, NY.

Pizer, S. (2012, March). *The analyst's generous involvement: Recognition and the "tension of tenderness."* Paper presented at the Harvard Medical School conference, Boston, MA.

Porges, S. (2009). Reciprocal influences between body and brain in the perception and expression of affect: A polyvagal perspective. In D. Fosha, D. J. Siegel, & M. F. Solomon (Eds.), *The healing power of emotion: Affective neuroscience, development & clinical practice* (pp. 27–54). New York, NY: Norton.

Prenn, N. (2009). I second that emotion! On self-disclosure and its meta-processing. In A. Bloomgarden & R. B. Menutti (Eds.), *Psychotherapist revealed: Therapists speak about self-disclosure in psychotherapy* (pp. 85–99). New York, NY: Routledge.

Prenn, N. (2010). How to set transformance into action: The AEDP protocol. *Transformance: The AEDP Journal, 1,* 1–29.

Prenn, N. (2011). Mind the gap: AEDP interventions translating attachment theory into clinical practice. *Journal of Psychotherapy Integration, 21,* 308–329. http://dx.doi.org/10.1037/a0025491

Prenn, N., & Slatus, J. (2014, January). *True self, true other, true other: Undoing aloneness and co-creating transformational experience in the therapeutic and supervisory relationships.* Workshop presented at St. Luke's Hospital, New York, NY.

Rizzolatti, G., & Craighero, L. (2004). The mirror-neuron system. *Annual Review of Neuroscience, 27,* 169–192. http://dx.doi.org/10.1146/annurev.neuro.27.070203.144230

Rodrigues, C., Conceição, N., Iwakabe, S., & Gleiser, K. (2015, June). *Voicing an AEDP supervision process: a case study on supervision session change processes.* Paper presented at the 31st International Conference of the Society for the Exploration of Psychotherapy Integration, Baltimore, MD.

Roisman, G. I., Padrón, E., Sroufe, L. A., & Egeland, B. (2002). Earned-secure attachment status in retrospect and prospect. *Child Development, 73, 1204–1219.*

Retrieved from https://www.researchgate.net/publication/11235443_Earned-Secure_Attachment_Status_in_Retrospect_and_Prospect

Rønnestad, M. H., & Skovholt, T. M. (2003). The journey of the counselor and therapist: Research findings and perspectives on professional development. *Journal of Career Development, 30*, 5–44. http://dx.doi.org/10.1177/089484530303000102

Russell, E. M. (2007, January 13). *Core training presentation.* Presented at the AEDP Institute, New York, NY.

Russell, E. M. (2015). *Restoring resilience: Discovering your clients' capacity for healing.* New York, NY: Norton.

Russell, E. M., & Fosha, D. (2008). Transformational affects and core state in AEDP: The emergence and consolidation of joy, hope, gratitude and confidence in the (solid goodness of the) self. *Journal of Psychotherapy Integration, 18*, 167–190. http://dx.doi.org/10.1037/1053-0479.18.2.167

Safran, J. D., & Muran, J. C. (2000). *Negotiating the therapeutic alliance: A relational treatment guide.* New York, NY: Guilford Press.

Sarnat, J. E. (2012). Supervising psychoanalytic psychotherapy: Present knowledge, pressing needs, future possibilities. *Journal of Contemporary Psychotherapy, 42*, 151–160. http://dx.doi.org/10.1007/s10879-011-9201-5

Sarnat, J. E. (2016). *Supervision essentials for psychodynamic psychotherapies.* Washington, DC: American Psychological Association. http://dx.doi.org/10.1037/14802-000

Schoettle, E. (2009). *A qualitative study of the therapist's experience practicing accelerated experiential dynamic psychotherapy (AEDP): An exploration of the dyadic process from the clinician's perspective* (Unpublished doctoral dissertation). Wright Institute, Berkeley, CA.

Schore, A. (2001). Effects of a secure attachment relationship on right brain development, affect regulation and infant mental health. *Infant Mental Health Journal, 22*, 7–66. http://dx.doi.org/10.1002/1097-0355(200101/04)22:1<7::AID-IMHJ2>3.0.CO;2-N

Schore, A. (2009). Right-brain affect regulation: An essential mechanism of development, trauma, dissociation, and psychotherapy. In D. Fosha, D. J. Siegel, & M. F. Solomon (Eds.), *The healing power of emotion: Affective neuroscience, development & clinical practice* (pp. 112–144). New York, NY: Norton.

Shohamy, D., & Adcock, R. A. (2010). Dopamine and adaptive memory. *Trends in Cognitive Sciences, 14*, 464–472. http://dx.doi.org/10.1016/j.tics.2010.08.002

Siegel, D. J. (2010). *Mindsight: The new science of personal transformation.* New York, NY: Bantam Books.

Stern, D. N. (1985). *The interpersonal world of the infant: A view from psychoanalysis and developmental psychology.* New York, NY: Basic Books. http://dx.doi.org/10.1176/ps.37.5.517

Stern, D. N., Sander, L. W., Nahum, J. P., Harrison, A. M., Lyons-Ruth, K., Morgan, A. C., . . . Tronick, E. Z. (1998). Non-interpretive mechanisms in psychoanalytic therapy. The "something more" than interpretation. *International Journal of Psycho-Analysis, 79,* 903–921.

Tomkins, S. S. (1962). *Affect, imagery, and consciousness: Vol. 1: The positive affects.* New York, NY: Springer.

Tronick, E. Z. (1989). Emotions and emotional communication in infants. *American Psychologist, 44,* 112–119. http://dx.doi.org/10.1037/0003-066X.44.2.112

Tronick, E. Z. (1998). Dyadically expanded states of consciousness and the process of therapeutic change. *Infant Mental Health Journal, 19,* 290–299.

Tronick, E. Z. (2003). "Of course all relationships are unique": How co-creative processes generate unique mother–infant and patient–therapist relationships and change other relationships. *Psychoanalytic Inquiry, 23,* 473–491.

Tronick, E. Z. (2009). Multilevel meaning making and dyadic expansion of consciousness theory: The emotional and the polymorphic polysemic flow of meaning. In D. Fosha, D. J. Siegel, & M. F. Solomon (Eds.), *The healing power of emotion: Affective neuroscience, development & clinical practice* (pp. 86–111). New York, NY: Norton.

Tronick, E. Z., Bruschweiler-Stern, N., Harrison, A. M., Lyons-Ruth, K., Morgan, A. C., Nahum, J. P., . . . Stern, D. N. (1998). Dyadically expanded states of consciousness and the process of therapeutic change. *Infant Mental Health Journal, 19,* 290–299. http://dx.doi.org/10.1002/(SICI)1097-0355(199823)19:3<290::AID-IMHJ4>3.0.CO;2-Q

Tugade, M. M., & Fredrickson, B. L. (2004). Resilient individuals use positive emotions to bounce back from negative emotional experiences. *Journal of Personality and Social Psychology, 86,* 320–333. http://dx.doi.org/10.1037/0022-3514.86.2.320

Wachtel, P. (1997). *Psychoanalysis, behavior therapy, and the relational world.* Washington, DC: American Psychological Association. http://dx.doi.org/10.1037/10383-000

Wallin, D. (2007). *Attachment in psychotherapy.* New York, NY: Guilford Press.

Watkins, C. E., Jr. (1997). Defining psychotherapy supervision and understanding supervision functioning. In C. E. Watkins, Jr. (Ed.), *Handbook of psychotherapy supervision* (pp. 3–10). New York, NY: Wiley.

Watkins, C. E., Jr. (2012). Psychotherapy supervision in the new millennium: Competency-based, evidence-based, particularized, and energized. *Journal of Contemporary Psychotherapy, 42,* 193–203. http://dx.doi.org/10.1007/s10879-011-9202-4

Watkins, C. E., Jr., Budge, S. L., & Callahan, J. L. (2015). Common and specific factors converging in psychotherapy supervision: A supervisory extrapolation of the Wampold/Budge psychotherapy relationship model. *Journal of Psychotherapy Integration, 25,* 214–235. http://dx.doi.org/10.1037/a0039561

Watkins, C. E., Jr., & Milne, D. L. (2014). *The Wiley international handbook of clinical supervision.* New York, NY: Wiley.

Watkins, C. E., Jr., & Riggs, S. A. (2012). Psychotherapy supervision and attachment theory: Review, reflections, and recommendations. *Clinical Supervisor, 31,* 256–289. http://dx.doi.org/10.1080/07325223.2012.743319

Winnicott, D. W. (1960). The theory of the parent–infant relationship. *International Journal of Psychoanalysis, 41,* 585–595.

Winnicott, D. W. (1965). Ego distortion in terms of true and false self. *The maturational process and the facilitating environment: Studies in the theory of emotional development.* New York, NY: International Universities Press.

Yeung, D. (2010). Transformance and the phenomenology of transformation: Self-transcendence as an aspect of core state. *Transformance: The AEDP Journal, 1.*

Yourman, D. B., & Farber, B. A. (1996). Nondisclosure and distortion in psychotherapy supervision. *Psychotherapy: Theory, Research, Practice, Training, 33,* 567–575. http://dx.doi.org/10.1037/0033-3204.33.4.567

Index

Qualitative research on AEDP,
  152–154

Receptive affective capacity,
    experience, 17–18, 24, 41
  expansion of capacity for, 39, 48
Recognition, 21
  "click" of, 11, 38
Recording, video. *See* Video
    recording
Reflection
  alternating with experience, 29,
      37–38, 45, 62–64
  in metatherapeutic processing, 5,
      10, 20–21, 32
Reflective skills, 67–70
Relational affects, 38. *See also*
    Transformational affects
Relational experience, 6, 31–34, 38,
    42, 100
  focus on, 50
Relational processes, 19–20, 49–53, 127
Relational skills, 59–62
  affirmation, 22–28
  ask permission, 19, 45, 113
  invitation to collaborate, 131
  relational metaprocessing, 131
  self disclosure. *See* Self disclosure
  "we-ness" language, 59–60
Repair, 10, 22, 59, 69. *See also*
    Attunement; Disruption
Research support for AEDP
    supervision, 141–154
  and accountability, 144–145
  and common factors in
      supervision, 145–149
  and excellence, 149–150
  and qualities of effective
      supervision, 142–144
  for transformative supervision,
      150–154
Resilience, 15, 144
Resonance. *See* Affective resonance

Resonance phenomena, 4
Responsiveness to need, 31–32
Right-brain-to-right-brain
    communication, 4, 48
Rigor without shame, 117–118
Risk-taking
  in case vignette, 92
  overview, 22–26
  and safety, 21
  secure attachment for, 6
Runnell, Gil, 5
Rupert, P. A., 148
Ruptures, alliance, 22, 146
Russell, Eileen, 5, 51–52, 156

Safety
  cocreation of, 17, 19, 91–92
  emotional, 6, 17
  and exploration, 6, 17, 21–22
  in group supervision, 119
"Saying all of it," 60
Scaffolding, 117
Schoettle, Elizabeth, 37, 130–131
Secure attachment
  in psychotherapy relationships, 6
  and self-disclosure, 61
  in supervisory relationships, 20
  undoing aloneness with, 26
Seeking system, 21
Self-awareness, 138
Self-care, 133–139
Self-disclosure
  as aspect of supervisory
      immediacy, 147–148
  in case vignette, 17–18, 101, 109
  and challenges in supervision, 131
  as common factor in
      supervision, 146
  function of, 17–19
  overview, 60–62
  and secure attachment, 6, 26
Self-experiencing self-disclosure, 60
Self-interruption, 58

About the Authors

Natasha C. N. Prenn, LCSW, is senior faculty at the Accelerated Experiential Dynamic Psychotherapy (AEDP) Institute. She pioneered the AEDP Essential and Advanced Skills Courses, and is well known as a trainer of therapists across the U.S. and abroad. In addition to her clinical practice in New York City, she offers individual and group AEDP supervision and runs supervisor trainings and writing groups. She is the founding coeditor of *Transformance: The AEDP Journal.*

Diana Fosha, PhD, is the developer of AEDP and founder/director of the AEDP Institute. She wrote *The Transforming Power of Affect: A Model for Accelerated Change* (2000) and coedited (with D. Siegel and M. Solomon) *The Healing Power of Emotion: Affective Neuroscience, Development & Clinical Practice* (2009). She has also written numerous articles integrating neuroplasticity, recognition science, and developmental dyadic research into experiential therapy and trauma treatment. APA has released two previous DVDs of her AEDP work. She lives and practices in New York City and teaches worldwide.